THE SECRET
LOVE
OF SONS

THE SECRET
LOVE
OF SONS

HOW WE MEN FEEL ABOUT
OUR MOTHERS,
AND WHY WE NEVER TELL

NICHOLAS WEINSTOCK

RIVERHEAD BOOKS
NEW YORK
1997

RIVERHEAD BOOKS
a division of G. P. Putnam's Sons
Publishers Since 1838
200 Madison Avenue
New York, NY 10016

Library of Congress Cataloging-in-Publication Data

Weinstock, Nicholas.
The secret love of sons : how we men feel about our mothers, and
why we never tell / Nicholas Weinstock.
p.   cm.
ISBN 1-57322-050-7
1. Mothers and sons.   2. Sons—Psychology.   3. Adult children—
Psychology.   I. Title.
HQ755.85.W47   1997
306.874'3—dc21   96-53191 CIP

Printed in the United States of America
1   3   5   7   9   10   8   6   4   2

This book is printed on acid-free paper. ∞

Book design by Chris Welch

For my mother,
naturally

CONTENTS

*Only the relationship to her son can bring a mother unlimited
satisfaction; it is in general the most complete, the least
ambivalent of all human bonds.*
—SIGMUND FREUD

Oh, what it is to walk in the dark!
—OEDIPUS

S PEAK TO A MAN ABOUT HIS MOTHER AND YOU WILL probably receive one of two reactions, both of them followed by an edgy silence. One is delivered with a shrug: "You kidding? She's the best. I mean, she's my *mom*. What do you expect?" The other is offered with a groan: "She means well and all, but what a pain in the neck. I mean, she's my *mom*. What do you expect?" And then comes the manly hush that is practiced and accepted throughout the world. When asked to discuss the women who gave us life, we find ourselves without language. Yet our silence is not the result of any lack of feeling, but rather of an excess. There are reasons for that reserve, and enough raw emotion and uncanny logic and personal insight trapped within it to fill volumes. This book was made possible by all I've learned in frank and private conversations with sons. It is based on the top-secret opinions of boys, and shaped by the startling reflections of men. But more than anything else, it is about our silence.

I suppose that most authors write books when they decide they know something uniquely. I was compelled to write this one when I realized that I did not. I had no idea how or why I'd let myself drift apart from my mother; at first it was hard for me even to see that I had. I sat next to her at family gatherings, called her on cue, even got her an occasional gift and answered one or two of her questions. Yet when it came to approaching her openly, I suffered from a paralysis that's common among young men and much more painful than it looks. In fact, the masculine mind-sets that have governed and separated me from my mom are nearly universal, and they are universally accepted with mixed feelings—but without much thought. As I have wriggled self-consciously away from the woman who used to hold me, I have been rocked by emotions that I've kept quiet. And so, it turns out, has every other son.

Of the hundreds of talks I was to have with men, my first two were with my younger brothers. Luke, at twenty-one years old, was eager to get cracking. He is talkative and sarcastic, an ex–football captain with a passion for debate. But as he positioned himself across the table from me, a pot of coffee and my tape recorder between us, it struck me that I had never seen him like this. He spoke about our mother softly, haltingly. There were snatches of true tenderness behind his armored wit. During the course of our three-hour talk, he waved the usual cigarette over his head, uttered the usual curses, cackled often, and punched the table, whirling through his opinions as my head spun to keep up. But then, for the first time that I can remember, he burst into tears.

Jake, three years older than Luke, was harder to corner. He is socially fluent in a way I've never mastered, eager and unegotistical, a man about town in places he's never been before. He agreed to the interview breezily, but was busy when it came time to turn on the recorder. He confirmed his willingness the following afternoon, then vanished just as I brought out my notebook. He laughed and nodded a day later when I brought it up once more, but he ran out of time before his evening plans intruded— and I ran out of patience. The next morning I climbed into his running shower with my list of questions. I stalked him with a loaded tape recorder as he dried and dressed himself, then I drilled him from the passenger seat as he drove to meet friends. Jake's responses—barely audible, when I played them back, over the drum of water and the roar of the engine—were pleasant enough, if rather curt. Two weeks later, he called me out of the blue. He felt like having lunch. No, it wasn't just that, he admitted. He had a good deal more to say.

If sons are erratic on the subject, it should not be surprising. Despite our instincts and education, men do not learn how to speak about our mothers. We admire and condemn our fathers as a matter of course, applying all that we learn about manhood to hoist them up, hack them down, and neatly reposition them in relation to ourselves. But for a man to spend that much time and energy on a mother would be odd, perhaps obsessive; a dalliance that she herself would discourage. Men are to find success among other men, not put it off by digging for hidden feelings and feminine sides. Sons are supposed to get busy making our moms proud, rather than making them the subjects of inquiry—or, certainly, of a book. But after years and generations of considering our mothers in secret, it is high time that we say what we feel.

For me and for all the other sons who have contributed, this book is neither the product of guilt nor a tool of blame. It's an investigation of our feelings, pure and simple, fun and complex. If all the baritone lore about men making their way through masculinity toward manliness rings a bit hollow, then a more honest analysis is called

4

for. And the reason it's never been conducted before is
that it's hard. Mother-son emotions resemble nothing else
and fit neatly into no context we know. The relationship
is a double crossover, combining all the closeness and distance between men and women with all the links and gaps
between parents and children. On one hand, our mothers are our most irrelevant onlookers, since no matter
what crooked and climbing paths we take in life, we will
never be moms. On the other hand, mothers are our first
and oldest friends, the coholders of an intimacy that will
not be equaled for the rest of our lives. Being a son involves a deft sleight of hand, as he must swallow his deep
and instant attachment to his mother in order to fend for
himself and thus please her. The mother of a son has a
job that's even more challenging: to prepare and rehearse
her child for manhood, the grave and crowded party to
which she is never invited.

Given the unique push and pull between sons and mothers, it is no wonder that our treatment of mothers is extreme.
The most soft-spoken homebody will lash out ferociously
against his mom; the very toughest guys among us turn to
mush in her presence. Even motorcycle-gang leaders wear
"Mom" tattoos, and pro-football players holler "Hi, Mom"
on television. But Hell's Angels are unlikely to call their
mothers from the road, nor do all-star quarterbacks want

them anywhere near the field. Men treat their mothers more callously and tenderly than anyone else they know. We live in terror of being mama's boys, but also in the fervent hope of honoring the women who gave us life. We want them off our backs and let them under our skins, but we very rarely tell them what's on our minds—even, and especially, when our thoughts dwell on our mothers themselves.

Take me, for instance. I've grown up scattered and straight, in the way that's expected of men. I have generally stayed out of trouble while not overstaying at home. My voice dropped on time, my grades stayed up in public and private high schools, I went to a big-name college and then a big office building in a big city. I've learned the value of money, gathered friendships and girlfriends, collected athletic scars and serious neckties, pursued enough foreign languages and far-flung adventures to settle down happily in my own place. And along with good manners and bad jokes, I have spent years honing another skill that's mandatory for men: the ability to set my mother lovingly aside.

It's a long story, with plot twists that have left both me and my mom in the dark until now. The development of a mother's son, in fact, is not one story but five: a miniseries that features tales of enchantment, of an emotional departure, of unspoken affection, of controversial romance, and, ultimately, of reunion. These are the five chapters of every man's life with his mother, realms of mystery and revelation that must at last be unveiled.

My first chapter, like everyone's, took place in the arms and under the sway of my mother. Free of full-family debates, safe from traffic, and cushioned from all hazards and pressures, I was content to depend on her and her guidance. She was a writer and editor in New York City and flexed her flexible schedule as far as it would go in order to take thorough care of me. While my father often worked in the murky world beyond our apartment, she and I made ourselves busy inside. Gradually, however, along with street noise and about the same time as school, something else began to filter in. More was expected of me. Challenges were orchestrated; my social and academic progress was tracked—all by my mother before anyone else. Slowly and unsurely, I followed her cues toward maturity and away from the intimacy of our secret garden. But that time and place now follow me as well, in flashes and feelings that I've kept to myself.

In the following chapter, my family moved to the square-lawn wilderness of southern Connecticut, and I moved away from my mom. I did not actually pack my bags and go, as ten is too young to head out—but too old to be devoid of thoughts of autonomy. Male independence had been somewhere on my mind, in fact, since the start. I had been born in late July of 1969, a few days after the first man set foot on the moon. From that summer on, talk of towering achievement and a vast and glimmering future was everywhere—and all of it seemed to be directed at me. As I worked to master Little League and first dates and geometry, I was surrounded by a cheering section: the one that rouses the ambitions of sons of all birthdays and backgrounds. In households and excited chatter all over the world, men's early lives are made out to be blastoffs toward glory. So I turned from my mother and set my sights up and away.

By the time I finished high school, the twinkling realm of manhood had hung over me for eighteen years. Macho self-sufficiency was sung about on the car radio, played out in every film I saw, and glorified by the woman who used to drive me to the movies. Thus it was striking to be on the brink of college life—and on the fence emotionally. My mother had encouraged me toward this third chapter for as long as I could remember, talking up collegiate culture at every turn until I shared her excitement and worked to bolster my typed application. I'd frantically edited the high school paper and the yearbook, played hard at four sports, took classes in three languages, and tutored anyone who happened to linger too long in the hallway. But now that I was finally on my way, my mom seemed ambivalent; and I was fully torn in two. Nonetheless, I was as determined as she was to keep up my progress and not to pause and turn myself inside-out. In deference to my fast-forming adulthood, we both managed to hide our raw sentiments away—and halt much of our communication in the process.

Those were not the only male-female emotions that I was keeping from my mother. Beginning years before my independence and continuing for years after, I secreted away an entire section of my life from her: a fourth chapter that includes all thoughts and feelings about romance. While my brothers have been more inventive when it comes to girlfriends, I've been something of a serial monogamist. However, not one relationship from my straightforward row has been the subject of an in-depth mother-son chat. As a man, I have refused to discuss women with my mom, although she happens to be an expert on the species and I've made a habit of discussing them with anyone else. The reasons for men's silence on the subject have been kept as hidden as their love lives. But both the reasons and our romances have more to do with our moms than either mothers or sons would guess.

My fifth and final chapter is only partly written. While

I've succeeded, halfheartedly, in separating from my mother—traveling alone throughout Europe and Africa, landing jobs at magazines and publishing houses under my own steam, living in apartments and styles of my own choosing—I am only just beginning to meet her once more. Nevertheless, it is a promising beginning. In the course of writing this book, I have conducted thorough interviews with nearly two hundred sons of various ages, races, opinions, and upbringings. The names of my sources have been changed, and identifying characteristics may have been altered to protect their anonymity. However, my mother's true character and unique identity have become increasingly clear to me as this project has progressed, and my most open and unprecedented contact has been with her. For a long stretch of years, I had assigned her to a sacred sort of irrelevance, revering and excluding her at once, and had banished myself to the thin, solo track that men are to follow. It's only lately that we both have reemerged to wonder at each other and at what in the world kept us secret.

Recently, my mother told me an odd story about myself. When I was little, she claims, I would end each day with a song, belting out a ballad once I was tucked in and left alone. The lyrics were always about the events of the previous twenty-four hours: *And then I played with the blue car, oh yes, and ran outside, and ran and ran, la-la, and Mum and Pops were mean to me . . .* until I would doze off somewhere after the eleventh or twelfth verse. Given the quality of my current singing voice, it's hard to imagine that this was a bedtime habit worth experiencing; yet my mother remembers standing outside my door with my father, muffling their laughter and waiting to hear if they would make it into the musical report.

If this book is my song—hopefully better orchestrated, and, thankfully, unsung—then for the very first time in my life, it is all about my mother.

—New York City, November 1996

CHAPTER ONE

THE SECRET GARDEN

L IKE A LOT OF GROWN SONS, I SPEND MOST OF MY visits home raiding the fridge, tugging at the bookshelves, cornering the cable television—and diligently avoiding my parents' drawer of old photos. It's the birthplace of boring stories, a sampler plate of arm-in-arm relationships gone sour. A sprawling museum of aesthetic mishaps, the photo drawer is far better left unentered. Therefore it seemed as good a place to start as any. I flipped through a few disorderly years. There was a wide-angle picture of my blond afro at ten years old, then a blurry action shot of my dad playing backyard quarterback. Another layer down I found a three-man team photo of me and my brothers dressed head to socks in identical red, white, and blue Olympic outfits. Finally I came

14

across a photograph of me with my mother. Just the two of us, for once, cleanly framed.

I almost slid it back in the drawer, then lifted it closer. Judging from the shine on my head and the chub of my splayed legs, I look to be going on two. My mother's face is upside down and inches from mine, smiling into my cheek as I grin directly at the camera. Her stance is devoted to her moon-headed son. Her long arms bracket my body; her necklace is a dangling toy. I am plunked down beside her with sheer delight in my eyes—which have swung away, drawn to the photographer instead. Looking at the picture now, I wonder at the game or gurgling conversation that had engaged us before we were interrupted. Which words, what fun made for the mother-son rapture that would soon become too hard, or else all too easy? The snapshot is evidence in black and white, and I stand awkwardly self-accused: once, my mother and I were wholeheartedly locked together. Somehow, with all those boyish glances around, I seem to have sprung our lock.

My mother and I are close. But when we see each other now, we both tend to be half-turned away toward our own affairs, arms and heads full, eyes roving. Our conversations often are frayed by attitude, garbled by background noise, chopped short. But how, and why? I wonder not for her sake but for my own, not out of guilt or good-heartedness but genuine curiosity. What happened to the vast easiness that sunshined between me and my mother, captured on film but elusive, somehow, in our lives?

The life of every single man begins not singly but with his mother. Baseball coaches and businessmen, artists and architects: we all were, at one time, mama's boys. Every analyst who watches a computer screen, and every farmer who watches the weather used to watch his mother's face the whole day long. Regardless of where or how we eventually grow up, our first years revolve around one woman, and she is our ticket back to them. A teenager tells me of his upbringing in China, where she used to carry him to preschool on her bicycle. A middle-aged man conjures his South American childhood through his earliest memories of her. Across the globe, scant years before kids give her the silent treatment, older boys hustle her off the phone, and grown men put off our visits home, a mother is our most vital companion. Cradled in that healthy and absolute dependence, sons keep the union private from fathers, siblings, and friends. And then, perversely, we they keep it from ourselves.

The closeness that's found in the photo drawer is not

foreign to me. I remember putting my small hands in my mother's big hair—curly, like mine, but always bent and smoothed into something finer, a neat bowl or sky-high bun that begged to be dissembled. I still can recall my first rope swing in the kitchen doorway, as well as the time I showed her how eating dog biscuits helped me to kick up higher. She taught me the French words for *orange juice* and *apple juice*; I taught her about the friendly population of inch-high aliens that I'd happened upon at a friend's house. My mother was more than a playmate: she was a fellow pioneer, since she knew as little about a man-in-progress as I knew about a full-grown woman. My tiny life was a wonder to her, just as her larger world held my wide-eyed interest and sparked my constant questions. We spent days and nights, weeks and months enlightening each other with tricks and stories. And now I have spent year after year thinking of those gentle sessions and stuffing them back away in my mind.

Although men tend to judge them inappropriate topics for adult conversation, they think of those early days all the time. Dave, now sixty years old, still sees them vividly: "My mother and I created what I imagined to be a kind of secret garden together," he says. "That was our relationship, and it was the innermost part of her life and the innermost part of my life. It was not in the text of what we said to each other; it was in the feeling and tone of that garden." Born in Europe, Dave was soon to experience the force of Hitler's Germany and the trauma of immigrating to America. But the tender era before all that remains pure in his mind. "That's where my mother and I were happiest: with each other," he says. "That's where life was softest and lightest and the most rosy-colored. It's where everything was beautiful. There was no death in that garden. There was nothing but each other." And Dave knew nothing but that garden for the first years of his life.

Most of the time, sons shove away this chapter as distant history. It's foggy, we insist, or irrelevant, involving us before we were really *us*. And that's true. For many of us, the details of that stage are distant. We know that she changed hundreds of our diapers but can't remember it, and we recall instead some street scene or backyard moment that she does not. I hold clear memories of melting sourballs to make stained-glass windows for our gingerbread house; however, many of the three-legged races, the walnut-shell-boat regattas, and the handmade Halloween costumes that my mom fondly created have seeped out of my leaky memory banks. My life with my mother contains loose ends and unlit corners—which only add to the shimmering ambiguity of our bond. I remember far more than I discuss, more than she'd ever think to ask about. Does everyone? Do all the boys and men who rush into the fray of school lives and working worlds carry that precious history along with them in silence?

Beneath the many and moving surfaces of each man lies a secret garden of his own. It is fiercely private, untouched since the time he lived there, undeserted although it's been left behind. As he grows, a son nourishes and maintains that intimate oasis in three ways: by celebrating its luxury, regretting its end, and reliving it in moods and moments he tells no one about.

The Apple of Her Eye

While all children can be made to feel special by a mother, young boys claim the extraordinary status of apple of her eye. And this rank is not something that we forget as we grow older. Our maleness created an entertaining distance between the two of us; our childish needs and curiosities closed that gap like a hug. As miniature men we played at grand independence, making our daily and hourly reunions with the women we depended on all the sweeter. Since we did not yet hate or fear girls and were light-years away from pursuing them, our mothers stood unbound by our future categorizations of females, spanning them all. In return, we wanted to be everything for our mothers.

It would be hard to say who, among the three of us, would be my mother's favorite son. In fact, it would be impossible—not only because of the hailstorm of punches and wisecracks that would follow, but because each one of us feels, deep down, that it would be he. I was born first, and therefore wondrously; Jake's birth was marvelously easy; Luke's was a perilous, premature delivery that may have glorified his arrival above ours. I provided my mom with her first opportunity to watch and understand baseball, introduced my pals as if presenting them to the queen, and won the English awards that made her proud. But it was Jake who was elected class president and who brought home bigger gangs of guy friends than mine, hordes of laid-back high schoolers who would pepper her with jokes and folklore about her son that must have pleased her more than prizes. And then came Luke to top us both, perhaps: the star player on more athletic teams than I'd even tried out for; the jovial host of team dinners that were more sprawling and celebratory than Jake's parties. From time to time, as we three have aged, we've even come up with gifts to cement our bonds with our mother: I've given her presents of secondhand books, Jake has bestowed scarves and blouses and other treasures from far-off lands, and Luke's cooked her gourmet meals in return for the dozens she cooked for the football squad. But it is not a race, of course, and we are not conniving to outdo one another. Why would we, when each of us knows he's been the winner all along?

Although I cannot speak about feeling special among sisters, Sam can: "My mother and I had a one-of-a-kind relationship when I was growing up," he says. "She and my sisters were at odds a lot of the time. They used to butt heads over issues that weren't relevant to a mother and a son." Maleness and motherhood combined to make Sam's upbringing unique, free of the friction between a woman and her women-to-be. While his sisters had to contend with their mother's views on femininity, for instance, as they struggled to dress, date, and act in their own style, Sam was at liberty to operate more impulsively around her—just as she was around him. "She would get really excited about my doing *boy* things," Sam says. "She loved that I played hockey and went on dates and put on little coats and ties and all that. She was just a fan, then, a friend who was happy to watch the show. We kept each other curious, I think." Not roped together by their gender, Sam and his mother had enough space to breathe easily and approach each other spontaneously.

However, sons do not roam through life without boundaries. Laws are to be made and enforced, and a mother is usually the first one to do so. Bedtimes and mealtimes, morals and manners: she is there to lay them all out and to monitor her son's performance. Boys commonly gripe about being saddled with rules and regulations, yet perhaps that's because they need them. We are boisterous and brash, fueled by testosterone and functioning at the mercy—and at the vanguard—of a worldwide trend of young male rowdiness. In fact, it's boyish yanking against mothers' limits that creates the fun and flirtation that sons enjoy with the woman in charge. We stick pencils up our noses, punch our brothers, pinch our sisters, and sprint around the house when it's time for our baths, laughing wildly until our mothers can't help but join us. In other words, sons can't lose. If we play by the rules, then we're golden; if we break them, well, then boys will be boys.

Perhaps the most resounding testimonies to that early

rapture are the private feelings of the men who never got to experience it. Harold is in his late fifties, a proud husband, father of three, and the head of a successful firm. Yet when he speaks in-depth about his mother, he becomes shaky: "I don't talk about her—ever. To anyone," he says. "This is hard. It's been years and years since I've felt exactly how I feel at this moment, talking to you. Which is . . . scraped. There's this horrible raw hurt that I used to feel all the time." There was no real abuse in Harold's family, nothing outrageous or criminal, but simply his mother's utter and voluntary absence from his life. She didn't care to know his friends, didn't attend his high school graduation, never asked about his interests before he grew up and pursued them. As a result, Harold felt completely alone. "My melodramatic story with my mother all stays within the box of seminormal, middle-class life," he says. "It's all subtle. She wasn't wicked, and she didn't beat me. She just was never there at all. She didn't care for me." Therefore, at our lunchtime interview decades later, Harold finds himself breaking down.

Carlos recalls the stark absence and unruly presence of his single, alcoholic mother, as well as the distress that her unreliability caused. After divorcing her Mexican husband and jumping bail on a drunk-driving charge, she moved around with her young son, making money as a waitress and spending it on drinking binges.

"I was left alone a lot when I was really young," Carlos remembers. "There was a lot of waiting by myself, outside bars, for hours. That I always resented—now, too, but especially back then. I never knew when it was going to end, and didn't know what was going on, and it was always really, really late at night. I just wanted a mom, you know?"

Carlos admits that he's always been confused by a mother who acted most often like she'd rather not be one: "It's kind of like this," he explains. "You have a garden. You do all these things for your plants, like make sure that they get the right amount of sun every day and that the soil is just the right composition for them to grow well. You tend them and get rid of the bugs and the weeds—and then every so often you just *stomp* on them. It was kind of like that with my mother and me."

Other sons suffer not from their mothers' absence, but from the absence of their mothers' affection. As luxurious as maternal pampering may be, sons do not consider it an extravagance. In the minds of the kids who have had to do without, it's a right. It's with outrage, for instance, that Drew recalls his mother's refusal to offer him any warmth or companionship thirty years ago, when he was small. Drew's mother was not invisible; however, she came as close as she could to being impassive. With his father working long days and nights as a police officer, she assumed the role of household disciplinarian, relentless and remote.

"I've always been upset about that," Drew says, "because I saw other families, other little boys and their moms, and there was that warmth there. I missed that. She insisted on being tough all the time, from the very beginning, and never in the least bit tender. I never got any personal attention at all from her. And that hurts, even now." With three boys to control and with law enforcement running in the family, Drew's mother avoided loosening up at all costs. And the effects of that policy still can be heard in her son's regret.

It takes extreme cases to inflict lasting harm, as mother-son unity is not fragile. The pain shared by Harold, Carlos, and Drew was not caused by their mothers' occasional oversight and was not the result of their professional overwork. A boy hardly needs a mother's relentless doting eighteen hours a day for eighteen years; he needs only to know that she cares for him. And while a son will hold all sorts of past injuries and negligence against the mother who may be responsible, he does not begrudge his mother's full-time job. At the time and in retrospect, working mothers do not lose their growing sons' fidelity.

"I never resented her for being a high-caliber professor," says Art. "I never felt a longing for more of a *mother*." Although Art was not judgmental, he can remember a parent-child day at preschool, twenty years ago, when his mother was put on trial. Parents were asked to come to the school to help with students' projects for the day; Art's mother, however, had to hire a baby-sitter to cover for her, and arrived only at the very end of the afternoon. "She came in just as everyone was going around the room, saying what they'd done with their kid and how it went and how they felt," Art says. "So when it got to my mom and she was asked what she had done to contribute to the group that day, she was frozen." At last, someone broke the tension by explaining that Art's mother taught college—followed by a long and wary *Ohhhhh* from the group. But from Art, then and now, his mother elicits a far more wholehearted response: "I've never cared about her fitting some old-fashioned, maternal mold. I was proud just sitting there with her in front of all the naysayers. I wasn't ashamed at all."

I'm fortunate that I had to interview other men in order to learn about the lack and limits of the secret garden. To me the garden felt boundless. My mother knew everything, including and especially me. We had friendship, humor, the glow of mutual discovery, and the thrill of glimpsing the rest of the world through each other. Before long, of course, a boy will glimpse things past his mother, discover people and issues that preclude their teamwork. Nevertheless, it's due to my mother's organic support that I have felt gifted all my life.

Sweet Sorrow

"Some part of me has always been astonished that the world is not as it was when there was only me and my mother," a middle-aged man confides to me. "And although one doesn't admit such things, it took me many years to deal with that difference."

Given the cushy treatment we receive in our gentle babyhoods, it is no wonder that our departures from there are jarring. Stepping beyond the shelter of our mothers, like walking out the door in winter, stiffens us up—hardening our stances, tightening our lips. And while we may peek behind ourselves at the glow of our beginnings, there is no turning back.

I recall my early years through a haze that adds to their softness. I used to be needy and show it without hesitation. She used to be infinitely wise and playful, the expert on me before I tried to be the expert on anything. Our communication was fluent and unbroken by the schedules and insecurities of growing men. And our bond was unshared, unbinding, and unmatched by any of the half-rewards that would mark the solo advance of the half-adult. In a few years, teachers and coaches would give me positive feedback when called for, but it would be nothing like the unmitigated encouragement that my mother used to supply. Sooner or later, friends would offer back-slaps and high fives, pale and hard in comparison to the warm support of an earlier time. When I glance back at them, the days of mother-son intimacy look and feel like the lap of luxury.

Trekking away from their mothers, many sons have had a rougher go of it than I have. And the harder "real life" has proven to be, the greater the secret longing for our softer lives in our mothers' company. Anthony spent time in various jobs, a few different states, and three drug-rehabilitation clinics before he settled down. Now sober and on break from his job in a bakery, he admits, "I think back all the time to those preadolescent years that I spent hanging around with my mom, when I was oblivious to work and money and drugs and how complicated things can get. That's when things were the way they were supposed to be." Life should be looser and healthier than it is for most men—and back then, it was. "I was a boy, and she was my mom," says Anthony. "I would go to school or go out to play, and I'd come home and there was that easy feeling of Mom being there. That's all there was to it, that easiness. That's what I remember."

Sons do remember more about their mothers, and about themselves under their care, than they choose to acknowledge. Like many of us, Edward lives with an unspoken dismay. "I know that my mother feels as if she's lost track, to some extent, of who I am," he says, "and I feel that way too, compared to the old days." Having just returned from two post-college years overseas, Edward is disconcerted. Although Edward is staying in her house, his mother complains that she hardly knows him anymore; and it's true that he had acted distant even before his travels made him so. During high school, Edward devoted himself to friendships and girlfriends and absented himself from home. Once in college, he called his mother seldom, and honest discussions were even rarer than that. Now, however, Edward regrets the development. "She sometimes says that she doesn't know what I've been feeling," he says, "not only for the last thirty months, but for a long time now. She wants to know what my emotions are and what's going on inside my head. And I try to share it—because, I guess, deep down I want her to know all that too. There never used to be all these negotiations and tensions between us. But I have no idea how to get back to the way it was with her before." Stumbling over that ignorance, Edward and other sons fall silent.

Growing up male, we are treated to a good deal of hoopla. School, sports, romance, and our other pursuits are encouraged and commemorated as rites of passage. Even our stallings and hard stretches can be glorified as manly struggle. But as we accelerate to the cheers and noise of spectators, we do not advance free of regret. While we work to construct and clutter our lives, we are not ignorant of what is commonly missing: the fluid and fulfilling relationship that grew between us and the very first person we knew.

Andrew is newly married, nearing the completion of his graduate degree, and generally content. However, he is secretly dismayed during every Hanukkah he spends with his mother. "My friends know what I like and what my interests are. But my mom will give me, like, a tie-and-handkerchief set that I'd never wear. I never say anything to her, but it saddens me. She's my *mom*. I mean, I want her, of all people, to know me." For many sons, presents and other props serve as handy measures of the closeness and gaps between them and their mothers. In Andrew's case, the distance that galls him is an inevitable result of changes in geography—and an unfortunate result of his not adapting to them. "When I lived with her, she knew what to get me for Hanukkah," he says. "Now I have to tell her all about my interests to give her some clue. And maybe I haven't done such a great job of it." By keeping his mother in the dark, Andrew has created his own legacy of awkward holiday moments and the private hurt that accompanies each one of them.

The holes that develop in mother-son relationships are particularly upsetting because we know that they upset our mothers and that we tore them ourselves. Over the course of his thirty-one years, Daniel has gone from suburban altar boy to urban folk singer. He complains that his mother doesn't appreciate his transformation: "She still wants to feel like, *Oh, I know my little boy*," he says. "But I think she's looked at me with kind of foggy glasses and has seen only what she wants to see"—or, more likely, what Daniel has allowed her to see. He admits to making scant efforts to keep her informed of his recent ambitions, using her ignorance as an excuse—but using his silence to keep her ignorant.

By excluding mothers from much of their ongoing lives, sons risk sealing themselves off from their moms and then missing them. "I startle her with my music and with the other things I'm into. She doesn't get what I want to make of myself now," Daniel says. "And that's distressing for both of us. Because I could definitely use more of her support." Daniel's mom is not devoted to his past identity; she has simply been given no way to progress with him beyond it. And the result, for son and mother alike, is disappointment.

Every boy retains a panel of experts whom he appoints, positions, and consults as he ages. And when he demotes his mother, turning instead to friends and strangers for advice, it is painful for them both. At one time, whether he needed feeding, changing, or a quick talk on a vast subject, his mother held all the answers. Now, on the contrary, he doesn't give her even the questions. This is how sons create the challenge and the sting of manly independence: a next stage in which they brave, halfheartedly, the bleaker world beyond their moms. The swords that we wield to clear some space for ourselves are double-edged, and hurt.

Going, Going

Not only do we sons remember and regret the changes of scenery as we shift into young manhood; we relive them. Leaving our mothers is so unsettling an action that it reverberates through us for the rest of our lives, despite our efforts to keep it muted. Aftershocks of that separation take us aback in vulnerable moments, and memories of the bountiful time just before the separation flood into our consciousness through an avenue we cannot block: our senses. Mother-son connections are supremely natural, more instinctive than intellectual, more strongly felt than effectively rationalized. So perhaps it should be no surprise, striking though it is, that so many men recall their earliest days with their moms in lush and sensory free associations.

For me it all goes back to sound, to the climb and topple of the pieces she would play on the piano. My slow childhood afternoons had a soundtrack in the rich patter that came from the living room. I would seek out the noise, slide up next to her on the glossy bench, and sit there, braced for action as if on a ride. And although the bench didn't move, everything else did. I remember watching her taut hands as they lifted and landed, checking her profile as it nodded regally, scooting down to watch her feet press the pedals. But what brings back those hours is not the efficiency of my memory so much as the spill of the music itself. At cocktail parties, in department stores, even on luxury car commercials, a few notes of classical piano can roll me back twenty years, straight to her.

Just as I am gripped by the music of museum receptions and Lexus ads, men all over the world are wrenched back toward their mothers in their minds. There is a motherward movement among sons of all ages, sparked by their subconscious and kept from the women they secretly reapproach. A business school student recalls the tone of his mother's singing voice as she used to put him to bed; a corporate executive still can smell the orange she gave him when he cut his four-year-old forehead; an elderly artist can describe the perfume his mother wore when he was an infant. Within their most private realms, uncluttered by overthinking, men are instinctively re-united with their mothers time and time again.

Before the mandates of men drowned out everything else, we were happily drowned in the sights, smells, and sounds of our mothers. But there is yet another sensation that returns from our early lives to clutch us: the sadness of leaving our mothers' sides. For boys, the garden gate swings open one way only, leaving us to reenact our stir-ring departure scenes over and over. Far behind us now, that traumatic move is far from forgotten, to our surprise and our discomfort.

We get better at it, of course. Boys spend years honing and practicing the act of simply leaving—after weekends, at the end of holiday visits, off to school, back to work. What older boys learn to conquer, though, is the open-ness of the struggle, not necessarily its pain. After even a quick telephone call or casual jaunt home in their twen-ties and thirties and forties, sons experience a poignancy that doesn't belong to the mundane situations that prompt it. Just going about the common lives of normal young men, we feel an arresting sadness carried over from an event we've put aside.

It washes over me more often than anyone knows. I feel oddly heavy-headed as I yank the car into gear. I throw another salute to my mother, who walks out to the garden with hedge clippers under her arm. She waves back, not longingly, and turns to lengthen her stride as if late for a meeting with the begonias. What's with me? I watch her straight progress across the lawn as I roll slowly down the drive. She's got things to do, a fully stocked life. She isn't wincing at my exit or even watching me go. And while I'm not hurting her—I'm only rushing back to the city to get some writing done before the week sets in so that I'll have a head of steam on Monday and won't screw up my schedule—I'm hurting. It's not my mother who's off-kilter: she's knee-deep in her neat, green rows already, getting on with her tasks. It's me. What's the dumb sorrow that leans on my chest, tugs my eyes to the rearview mirror as I finally roar away?

Trevor is always speeding off as well, although his routine is far more glamorous than mine. A fashion model in his early twenties, he has exotic photo shoots, international runway shows, and something that drags him down unexpectedly at the beginning of each trip: "My mom is guaranteed to get a little choked up right before I go," he says, "even if it's just a month-long modeling stint. And I get moved too. It's hard to explain; it's just a certain mood. I'm like, *This is* Mom, *and I love her,* you know?" Few would guess that men with Trevor's looks and lifestyle could have trouble leaving their mothers. Personally I am almost disappointed to hear it from him. Yet Trevor explains that it's not that simple: "It's not that I don't want to go," he says. "And she's not saying, *Don't leave me.* She's just saying, *I hope you'll be okay.* But it cuts kind of deep, for some reason." In fact, it has little to do with reason, but rather with the emotional allegiance to their mothers that men on the go try endlessly to leave behind.

The same refrain is sung in popular music, classical literature, religions of the world, and most of our social circles: Sons must break away from mothers to get anywhere. But what nobody teaches us is that it's grueling. *What, you miss your mommy?* the guys razz. Of course not; we are plenty strong. We do and state and feel things strongly—including something for our mothers that we are not supposed to admit. The truth is buried beneath years of effort and layers of toughness: Our pursuits, as masculine and appropriate as they may be, yank us from our mothers long after they're supposed to.

When Tom entered the armed services at nineteen, on the brink of the Gulf War, it was not unexpected that both he and his mother were a bit undone. More remarkable is the sentimentality that accompanies each of his civilian departures now. "She still gets sad about me, and I do about her," he admits, "even though we don't say anything like that. When I go up to her house for a weekend these days, I'll be fixing to leave and she'll start to have a tear come to her eye. Funny thing is, I feel it too." Tom is married and happy to be living and working a few hours from his tiny hometown. However, before he leaves his mother, he finds himself dawdling in the kitchen, asking her another question or two, putting off his trip out to the car and to his own home. "I guess I feel like she might be unhappy to be stuck there," Tom considers, "and I might be unhappy to be out of there." But these are two questions that go unspoken and thus unanswered, as neither Tom nor his mother wants to keep him dwelling at home too long.

The pang of seeing and leaving their mothers is no knock at men's success and does not contradict their contentedness. What rattles us is the shaky sense that we're neglecting something we care about. In an effort to quell it, we bolster and steady ourselves with hearty helpings of male mythology. Valiant blokes throughout history have strode away from weeping mothers in order to go forth and triumph. Nothing ventured, nothing gained, as no one would deny. Sons shall break their mothers' hearts to break new ground. But such slogans fall flat when simple leave-takings swell with emotion that we can hardly explain and that suggest a resounding heartbreak of our own.

Our whole world changes when we leave our mothers' sides. The domains of baby boys are governed by feelings, not by outside orders or circumstances. But a more adult life is landscaped by practicalities and merely clouded or warmed by passing emotions. Back then, to need a mother ensured a central, fulfilling bond. Now it suggests some lack of masculine fulfillment. This vast and drastic shift represents a change of contexts, however, not a change of heart. Sons do not up and decide to take off. The companionship of mothers and sons is neither abandoned by boys nor invaded by other parties; it is quietly shaken by the cues and hints of mothers themselves.

Out of the Garden

The friendship that I built immediately with my mother—on beaches and lawns, crib floors and piano benches—remains unparalleled in my far-flung travels ever since. In fact, most men fumble for the rest of their lives to achieve the sort of intimacy that grew between baby boys and their mothers. So why put it aside? If we are destined to rejoice in our memories, regret our self-separations, and relive scenes and aspects of that all-too-brief era, then what's our hurry to leave?

The call to grow up and out is rarely a joyous one. It's less of a trumpet blare than a chorus of muttered clues that come first, and often accidentally, from a mother. It is our mothers who open the garden gate, not only letting us go but actually ushering us out with a series of small revelations. Our wholehearted twosomes are cut short by the dawning awareness that our moms have not been completely up-front with us. Well before we learn the art of reticence, we catch our mothers withholding at least two schools of information: their anxieties and ambitions for us as their children, and their own social lives as independent adults. Uncovering these foreign realms in our own maternal backyards, we become eager to research the rest of the world firsthand.

For a little boy, it is a shock to discover that smuggled within his mother's love is a sharp and rational child-raising strategy. As he looks back, this domestic policy of hers is likely to make a lot of sense; yet its disclosure at the time is chilling. His mom has been directing his progress all along. His kindly provider has an agenda, and even if it's for her son's sake, it's as staggering a discovery as traffic lights in the leafy repose of the secret garden.

Both utter trust in my mother and all musical ambition were wiped out when I declared that I hated my piano teacher—and my mother still made me report weekly to Mrs. Muldoon. "But she's *mean* to me," I would insist, as if this bombshell must not have been heard the first four times I dropped it. "Well, then, you should *practice*," my mother would chirp. To her, the world was divided into boys who learn to work hard and those who never do. My world was strictly divided as well: good versus evil; tossing a brand-new baseball or slogging through clumsy scales; me against Mrs. Muldoon and a growing army of unfairnesses. And my mother—supposedly for my sake— had defected to the other side.

Darren's cold realization, at eight or nine years old, was different from mine. Rather than shoving him out into meanness, Darren's mother, he suddenly noticed, was keeping him in the dark. He got the picture as he over-heard his mother's phone conversations with his teachers, his baby-sitters, and her friends: she was plotting his life without his input.

"Of course, your mother's right," Darren now says from the perspective of a thirty-five-year-old considering children of his own. "She has to be careful with you when you're small. She has to be good about what she discloses and how she guides you. But on the other hand, you look at her back then, as soon as you pick up on that, and you feel like she's *acting*. You realize that she's following a script, and that's a truly regretful feeling." We bristle at the idea that our mothers may not be letting us in on our own upbringings, or letting us know all about the money, labor, and arrangements that go into them. "I wanted to be treated with full disclosure by her," Darren says. "That was an awful part about being a little kid. I suddenly knew that she was thinking more and different things about me than she told me directly. It felt like a betrayal."

The betrayal may be perceptible only to little boys; but in their eyes it's dramatic. We are stunned to discover that our mothers have not only covert plans for us but their own secret lives. They have private errands and personal belongings and evening engagements that sons—the apples of their eyes, for heaven's sake—are not let in on. And in return, boys keep their reactions under wraps. A son's hidden knowledge of his mother's hidden knowledge is tucked away quickly, buried beneath smiles and talk and household distractions. But it grows almost daily and soon is impossible for boys to ignore. More mature judges see no crime: every woman attempting to raise a man should, of course, work from some sort of blueprint. In the eyes of young sons, however, the secret garden and their moms' not-so-secret efforts to mold them seem outrageous opposites.

It's hard, I would imagine, for any laboring parent to keep a poker face in front of children. But for a woman competing against male mind-sets and juvenile attitudes in the same small person, it must be all the more easy to tip her hand. Brent's mother, he came to find out, had specific ideas on how to grow a son. She pushed him toward sports and activities in which he had little interest, and avoided all conversations that seemed girlish or indulgent. "She had a very clear sense of what would be good for me and bad for me when I was little," says Brent. "She didn't want me to be too much of a homebody or lack toughness." Therefore, she carefully arranged his plans with playmates, convinced him to take up football like other boys in his class, and shooed him out of the house whenever she could. What gradually dawned on her only son was that his mother didn't have his interests in mind as much as his rate of development; and with this realization came the urge to dart out on his own.

"She gets sad now when I'm never around," Brent says.

"But she's forgetting that she used to push me to do things on my own. Did she expect me not to catch on?" When life is new and strange, and even the best of fathers tends to come and go daily, a mother is the foundation. And when that foundation shakes a son he finds himself sprinting for the door.

Eric's mother is something of an urban hero and clearly his primary role model. Having grown up with three younger siblings and no father figure, he boasts that he was "more my mom's partner than just her kid," and the two still speak at least once daily. Despite this closeness, or more likely because of it, Eric felt stung by his mother as he prepared to go to college. Struggling to provide for four children in a violent neighborhood on little income, she suddenly revealed the pragmatism behind her parenting. "Once I finished high school, *bam!* That was all she could help me with," Eric says. "College, sure—if I could get through it on my own. But there was nothing she could really do there, financially or otherwise. I was off." His mother had to refocus attention and resources on getting three more kids through secondary school, a perfectly rational maneuver that left her oldest son wounded. "It was hard to hear that from her," Eric says, "and hard to have her cut off all my money, to be honest.

You think your mother's your everything, you know, and then she turns out to be pretty cut-and-dried about matters. Now, though, I see that it's one of the dopest things she did, because it taught me to grow up and be a man." Eric's emphatic autonomy, as he nears his college graduation, was not his idea as much as his mother's. Though it's macho for a boy not to rely on a female provider, his manliness is often forged by his mom.

In my case, I had to be hit over the head with social independence, weekend after weekend, before I learned its brutal meaning. Teetering on the cliff of the very top stair, I stood in between worlds in my pajamas. Below, my parents' dinner parties bubbled and crashed like a fantastic waterworld. After long minutes of plate-clanks and murmurs, I'd hear the rise of my mother's voice, laughing with an abandon I hadn't witnessed, making a point I couldn't fathom, and my solid sense of her loyalty would tremble. It was rocked further by the sight of her lit and painted face, as she emerged for more carrots or wine, slowly turning to dismay as she spotted me. I was not the guest of honor here. Her padded shoulders would slump, and her bright eyes would fall as she walked over: not to tug me into the festivities or chortle at my jokes, but to sternly send me away. Such hard and vivid moments, piled together over time, constituted a simple lesson—

and a son's second prompt out of a mother's influence. People are not absolutely everything to each other. A one-and-only mom and her precious baby boy make a lavish, loving twosome. But we are not, it becomes clear, the whole, real world.

That world, for instance, involves work. When Drew trooped along with his mother to her job as an office manager, he was startled by an entirely different aspect of her personality. "The first thing that hit me was that she really laughs," he says. "When she's among her colleagues and other women, she's *fun*. And she was never that fun at home when I was growing up." Managing three little boys, Drew's mother had little time for off-the-cuff merriment. Therefore, as he watched her socialize among adults, Drew was struck by her enjoyment of the mob of life beyond him. "Seeing that opened me up in a lot of ways, in terms of her," he considers, "but not necessarily *toward* her." It was toward the rest of the world that Drew was abruptly swiveled, his interest in unmotherly entertainment having been heightened for good.

A partnership between sons and mothers is born when we are and is confirmed in wordless moments for the rest of our lives. However, every partnership is comprised of two distinct people, and every boy must learn this in order to grow up. That a mother acts carefully and selectively around him is curious; that she has a whole spectrum of other activities that she actually *enjoys* is something of an outrage. It's just common sense, looking back on it; but what we sensed back then, as small boys looking forward, was that the secret garden is limited. If people and situations beyond our sights can engage our mothers, making them scheme behind our backs, stay out late without us, and laugh out loud—well then, frowning and abruptly ambitious, we'd better go see things for ourselves.

CHAPTER TWO

UP AND AWAY

As I ascended to double-digit ages, my treatment of my mother descended in the grip of my small, iron fist. I slammed doors, raised my voice as it cracked lower and lower, handed down merciless decrees on everything she did. My mom was allowed to drive me to the movies but not sit in my row, buy me clothes but not advise me on which ones, help me arrange dates but not ask me a thing about them afterward. My ferocious distance seems as shocking to me in retrospect as it must have been to my mother at the time. Now older, slightly sheepish, and increasingly curious, I can't help but try to understand: How had I gone so swiftly from adoring my mother to ignoring her?

The only way to get behind the sudden tyranny of preteens and teens, I figured, was to interrogate the tyrants themselves—so I gave a questionnaire to the male students currently attending my old high school. It was fun to recognize the classes, teachers, and social events mentioned in their responses, funny to remark on how little had changed. And it was suprising to see a familiar trend when it came to mothers. A handful of the boys' answers, listed in order from seventh grade to senior year, speak for themselves—and for so many teenage guys standing awkwardly apart from their moms.

I will never talk to her about my personal life, like girls and friends.

I would like to tell her to let me deal with my own life!

I want her to leave me the hell alone! And please stay away from my stuff.

She is always asking about everything about my life. I don't have time for that.

She should leave me alone and mind her own business.

She has to leave me to do my own thing—I'm no moron.

Let me make my own decisions.

LEAVE ME ALONE!!!!

I know the outbursts and exclamation points well, as all these responses once belonged to me. I remember giving these stiff-arms without giving reasons—which is to be expected. When it comes to separating so fiercely from his mother, a son's reasons are even more evasive than he is; and his feelings are still harder to find.

The reason boys are so hard to track is that they're set in blurry motion even before they can walk. As men of the future, we are quickly convinced we have destinies over the horizons and the masculine power to zoom ourselves there. Our homes are carefully tended, our sights lifted, and our trajectories watched closely, all by a mother more than anyone else. By encouraging her son to soar, she inspires him to accept the mother-son gaps that grow as he does, as these are signs of upward progress. However, his departure is hardly painless. A son defends his own space and freedom confidently, since his mother has launched him earnestly into it; but not without his doubts. Boys' decisions to be single-minded and standoffish are made far more obediently than spontaneously, as they are propelled, in small steps and giant leaps, to a distance from their mothers that's both impressive and sad.

The Boosting of Boys

As little boys, we're convinced we can do anything. And while our self-certainty may be a bit inflated, it does not seem groundless. After all, we're surrounded by presidents and superstars who not that long ago were mere boys themselves. We're assured by wise adults that if we just do our homework and drink our milk, we'll grow up smart and strong like the macho celebrity of our choice. The path to manly success is elucidated by teachers, yelled about by coaches, and flashed constantly on television and movie screens—but it's lodged in our minds, first and firmly, by our mothers: Watching her boy dig around the backyard, she proclaims his future as a renowned archeologist; in her boy's deft argument against bedtime, she foresees a career as a top-notch lawyer. Daughters, too, can and should be cheered toward such heights; but given our dearth of female presidents and multimillion-dollar moms, such talk may be less popular. For young men, for better or worse, the sky's the limit. And their mothers are their most powerful boosters.

More than anything else, a mother fuels her son with faith. The comfort of the secret garden becomes more personalized and urgent as she moves from peering over him to get behind him and push. However gentle that support, the goals are astronomical. A friend of mine heard from his mother, at seven years old, that he was destined to write the great American novel. Another, as a promising teenage actor, was assured by his mom that he was the next Robert DeNiro. And another, just starting voice lessons, was led to believe that he was on his way to being Elvis. Other children are infused with daydreams as well—the sisters of Robert and Elvis were prodded to greatness on their own terms—and other people are sure to provide them with hard knocks and humility in time. From their mothers, however, boys get early, inspiring glimpses of the towering destinies before them.

James pays the highest tribute to his mother's boost: "She taught me from minute one that I was God's gift to mankind." He laughs. "And there's no way I would have achieved what I have without that. That was her gift."

Coming from a single-parent household of small financial means, James faced a long series of hurdles before he could become the successful young lawyer he is today. He applied to law school three times, faced the skepticism of teachers and friends, and heard only one voice that constantly urged him on. Without his mother's brisk sendoff, James, like a lot of men, might have been worn down before he got where he is. As boys grow up, they are taken down rung after rung until they are hardened, realistic, and pushed to fend hungrily for themselves. "That's how I've gotten through things," James agrees. "I've taken on a lot of odds and been knocked back time and time again. And if I didn't have my mom to get me thinking about the reward that's past all that, then I don't know whether I could have toughed it out."

Mothers create momentum, shooting their boys over all barriers in the way. "One of the problems with growing up in such a small town," reflects Edgar, "was my so-called *specialness*." The oldest of three boys and clearly gifted as a child, Edgar needed "special attention"—accelerated classes and more challenging schoolwork that were not readily available in his local school system. It was his mother, a part-time real estate broker, who campaigned for the sake of her son and his education. She tutored him at home on subjects not offered in the third grade; she encouraged the school to hire an algebra teacher in the fourth grade; she coached him on the social repercussions of skipping the fifth. Now in his mid-twenties and already a partner in a powerful financial firm, Edgar considers her efforts gratefully: "She borders on being over-involved with my younger brothers, and probably was with me too," he considers, "but without that kind of dedication, it's likely I would have fallen between the cracks."

When a mother's doting turns to ambition, however, many boys are jarred by it. Her nudge from behind is meant to prompt a high-reaching son even higher and farther; but some boys are not yet headed that way and are shoved out of the nest backwards. Face-to-face with a mother's momentum instead of a healthy distance before it, we are impressed by its strength and bruised by its impact.

When I became a teenager I took off, for a month, on a ragtag bicycle tour across France. After my safe summers of day camp, dishwashing jobs, and public beaches, my mother was pleased to see me head out for a more challenging landscape. As the youngest in the bike troupe, I was excited as well—mainly to have chocolate croissants for breakfast and to discover that my spindly legs could grow actual muscles. Then came the afternoon when my ten-speed, my leg muscles, and I barreled into a parked car somewhere north of Paris. Frowning and prodding my cuts and bruises, the *médecin* left it up to me: I could take a few days off to heal, or else head home. Personally, I was leaning toward home. The pleasant shudders of my first grand leave-taking had worn off on impact with the automobile, leaving only a sharp and hollow need for my mom. But I can still hear her transcontinental insistence, as I juggled francs into the pay phone, that I see this trip through, do what I set out to do, don't quit. I was hurt and homesick—but not bailing out, if she had any say in the matter. Her firm speech had greater scope than a summer and spoke of loftier ambition than bike riding. She was behind me for life; just so long as I was going forward.

Adam, among others, has a similar story. Buoyed by his mother's enthusiasm and caught up in his own dreams of athletic prowess, he signed up for a lacrosse clinic in third grade. It wasn't until his mom had driven him to the field that Adam balked. "All of a sudden, I thought, *Whoah, what am I doing?*" he recounts. "I didn't know the first thing about lacrosse, I didn't know any of the kids who'd signed up, and I was like, *I'm not getting out of the car.*" Faced with the choice and struck by the contrast, Adam couldn't imagine leaving his mother's side for the foreign and competitive arena a few yards away. But his mother did not allow him to choose. At the time, her toughness took him aback. "She was like, *We paid your seventy dollars for the clinic, you wanted to do it, and now you're doing it.* But part of me was thinking, *What about your poor little kid, here, who doesn't want to leave you?*" Within a few days, of course, Adam had immersed himself in the sport; and within a decade, he would play lacrosse for one of America's top-ranked college teams. Before he was banging shoulder pads with star players, however, he had to be pushed out of his comfortable seat by the mother who owned it.

A boy's life is a big deal, so big that a mother's individual effort may not be enough to get it going. To broaden her boost, she assembles and makes use of the whole family and of a family's wholeness. Just as a mother once fine-tuned her baby's environment to his needs—warming bottles, mashing food, cueing excitement and calm when necessary—she now juggles many elements of a household for his sake and for his future. She is the founder and facilitator of his home life, no matter what she may do outside the home. And the more work she puts into his be-

ginnings, the clearer she makes her motivation: to or-
chestrate the sort of healthy start that can serve as both
springboard and safety net as a son tries to make it on his
own.

My mother's quick comments and offhanded remarks
braced me against my family and pointed me upward. She
assured me that situations still over my head would some-
day make me grateful for my upbringing. She insisted it
would be to my ultimate benefit to learn all that European
history by test time, to get used to sharing with my brothers, and not to get the newest Adidas high-tops the split
second they landed in stores. One by one, my mom
promised the expiration of all her virtuous bans, making
grown manhood sound like a fantastic place where Flint-
stones cereals pour freely, cursing is just fine, and nobody
stops anyone from gaping at sixteen hours of television a
day. The future is all mine, I was convinced as a little boy.
But the home environment that would send me there
was in the hands of my mother.

Such catapulting backgrounds are constructed with
solid effort and ideas. A father knows, from personal experience, that boys tend to turn out okay; my mother was
far less comfortable leaving anything to chance. While
physical chores, for example, were not an organic part of
a kid's life in New York City, my mom made sure we

walked all over, learned to fix appliances, labored enough to do ourselves good. Intellectual exertion was mandated as well: heedless of our dragging feet, she pulled us through museums and shepherded us into libraries. But spirituality was the key ingredient that she feared missing. Our Jewish and Christian parents seemed to have canceled each other out, leaving a perilous gap in our worldviews. So she bustled us off to church on holidays for semiannual field trips in the realm that we might otherwise lack.

Every Christmas and Easter, my mother's boys slumped in straight-backed pews as if sentenced to holy time. In the name of our extracurricular education, we faked the lyrics of songs we'd never learned and hymns we'd never heard, even murmured each time the rest of the flock moved their lips. With Jake acting out lynchings with his necktie and Luke whispering about how much loot was on that plate, we groaned and giggled in houses of worship just like we complained on long walks and whined in the Guggenheim. Yet gradually, despite our antics, all three of us were beckoned by the all-powerful beyond. We were being shaped and primed for the rest of our lives, and as this revelation sank in, we grew impatient to get there. Fidgety in church, restless at the dinner table, and sulky at family obligations, we came to want above all what our mom wanted all along: for her sons to advance beyond her training in body, mind, and soul.

Tight families and well-engineered home lives do indeed work. Sons feel grateful, years later, once they've made use of them; but it's mothers who see the whole picture first, planning and trusting the effectiveness of household harmony, weighing its importance—and even tilting the scales in its favor. Case studies and therapy sessions have proven it over and over: young men need a launching pad. And in order to invent one, mothers may choose to blur any faults, hiding all cracks, divots, and shortcomings. Perhaps it's justifiable. Anything, I suppose, to aim their sons higher. Yet such superficial repair work is resented by the boys who are sent off with false smiles.

It's hardly an accident that Wallace is pursuing a Ph.D. in family psychology. As he was growing up, his household was in disarray, wracked by his father's infidelities and his mother's cancer. Yet his mother seemed just to will the strife away. In her conversations with friends and acquaintances, she took care not to let people penetrate an attractive picture of things in the household. Even with family members such as Wallace, she was noticeably guarded. "She seemed to care a lot more about appearances than me, my father, or my brother," he says, "and it seemed to be for her sons' protection. I didn't find out about all the troubles until much later." Although inevitably he became aware of his mother's illness, Wallace could not get her to discuss her marital strife or her consuming sadness, offering a rosy—if rather blank—portrait of their home. While the secrecy may have been useful for Wallace's sake, it was painful for him too. "I wanted the whole story," he says. "I felt, and still feel, that I deserved to know it all from her." In an effort to be a good mother, she steered Wallace away from an ugliness that might bog him down. But with a keen desire to be a good son, he has always been insulted by that effort.

In truth, the pain of sons is inevitable. No matter how tidy, supportive, or straightforward our homes, disengaging ourselves from our mothers hurts deeply. Even and especially in the best of family circumstances, detaching from the woman who arranges them is less of a clean ejection than a tearing away. It is a common and forbidden theme in our ambitious life stories, a well-hidden secret of all sons that our takeoffs temporarily wreck us as well.

Burned by the Launch

As growing boys, we are very conscious of our separations from our mothers before, during, and after their occurrences. But while the suffering of deserted moms is world famous, the grief of the deserters is unmentionable. Even those of us inclined to voice our unease are dissuaded by a litany of old sons' tales. We're told that a mother's discomfort, beginning with childbirth, is built into the experience of having sons. We're assured that in a full-throttle departure, leaving some wreckage is a customary part of the show. These sayings serve their purpose, focusing public attention on a mother's heartache and away from her son's. But they are more popular than convincing and do little to settle the disturbing paradox at the heart of every boy's relationship with his mother: Sons create pleasure and pain by moving on.

Bitten hard by the travel bug, I decided to follow my summer of full-contact cycling with a low-budget, high-risk hiking trip to Newfoundland. I could barely contain my excitement as I broke in my boots on our staircase and practiced pitching tents in the den. My mother understood my fourteen-year-old urge, being something of an outdoor explorer herself. But when she drove me to a parking lot to meet my fellow trekkers, most of whom had full beards, there was something lingering between us besides the spirit of adventure. As the rusted-out tour van coughed and creaked away, I felt it more strongly: an invisible rip below my eager surface.

For those few weeks I was thrilled to be roughing it, man-style, far from my cushy home. I lugged canoes, chugged down instant soup mix stirred into cold water, knocked slugs off my sleeping bag, and conked out. But in stream after white-water stream, I felt a deep pull from somewhere familiar. While gazing up nightly like the modern cowboy I fancied myself, I was dazzled by the webs of stars—but caught by flickers of sadness. I missed my mother. I longed for the solid sense of comfort that was her specialty, for the friendship that was ours. It was an enormous need, larger than the vista and harder than anything. And it was exactly as it should be. My mixed feelings were what made that rite of passage profound. Tender thoughts of my mother cut through my leathery teenage ego and stung, toughening me deeper and quicker than my daily blisters and rashes. By the time I got back home, I was seasoned. And more than any of the perils I bragged about loudly upon my return, it was that unrevealed hurt that had made my voyage heroic.

Every boy has his own heralded coming-of-age ceremony. For Ralph, it was football camp. He had just entered high school, and it was time to make more of a commitment to things. His mother was as excited as he was when they went to the bus station together at the beginning of the summer, and both of them grinned goodbye on cue. But by leaving, it turned out, Ralph wounded them both. "When we were driving off, my mom cried and cried," he says. "She's a strong black woman and all, and she knew I'd wanted this forever, but she was a waterfall." If Ralph was surprised by her reaction, he was blindsided by his own. During the next month, he dreamed about his mother frequently, waking up strangely sad. He had plenty of friends and even a girlfriend at camp, keeping his mind and body busy; but amid all the activity, Ralph's summer felt halfhearted. Nevertheless, he kept up appearances, kept up with his fellow campers, and eventually celebrated the time spent on his own. "I loved that camp," he says, "and even though it was hard to leave my mom, you can't show that shit. You keep it in and you do your thing. I mean, I was playing *football* and it was supposed to be *my* time and all that." Therefore Ralph fell into line, like squad after squad of growing men before him, and swallowed the thoughts that preceded his training in toughness.

A son is struck not only by the potency of a mother's

support but by the direction it nudges him: away, most often, from her. The lofty dreams she puts in our heads cannot be played out in her living room. The home life she gathers and bolsters is geared to help us thrust ourselves great lengths from that home. Boys realize this and recover quickly, leading their own charges into their own futures. But their starts in life are often stuttering and ambivalent, regardless of how they may appear. Sooner or later, a son accepts and even embraces his role as boundless adventurer, as well as a mother's role as the one who watches him go. But for him to get to that point requires an arduous and unspoken journey.

What may seem our inborn need to separate is learned over time—and from the very women we often injure by doing so. William, for instance, was very close with his mother until he was fifteen. She had quit her job to have children, and as he grew up he avoided rowdier activities in order to spend time around the house with her. "I was the Home Boy," he admits. He refused to swipe money from his mother's purse the way his friends did before video arcade outings; he spent his weekend nights in the house, routinely telling his mom all he could about classes, friends, and passing fancies. But when William's departure for boarding school loomed, her gentle pull became a gentle push. "My mother had made it clear, by the time I was about to leave for tenth grade, that no matter how sad she might feel about it, deep down she wanted her boys to go out and conquer," he says. "She'd actually say that kind of stuff, even when we were little." When such rallying calls are heard first at the age of three, they must seem nonsense and the last thing a boy would want to do. Yet by the time older boys have heard it over and over, they are already beating their mothers to the punch. Once William was at boarding school, his calls and visits home became increasingly rare. Focusing so hard on conquering, he had little time to fill his mother in on the details of the process; so grades, social events, and girlfriends became confidential. Once his constant companion, William's mother had begun to urge his constant progress as an individual. And with startling speed, her son caught up with the redirection.

If a boy can no longer look his mom in the eye, it's because she set his sights, long ago, on the rest of the world. To turn from a mother is difficult and distressing and is made only harder by her calls for his attention. Sons must step away from such entanglements to clear their paths toward adulthood. In order to endure the private uproar of leaving home, we must close ourselves off and batten down the hatches, keep things staunchly to ourselves and shoo away our mothers. Our behavior can be brutal, and our stone-throwing and stonewalling may astonish our mothers. However, those actions are no mystery: they match the mother-son turmoil that is ongoing deep within us.

Even in the throes of adolescence, Brian was conscious—and self-conscious—as he established a rift between himself and his mother. Self-removal may seem cruel at the time, but to sons it seems inevitable. "Kelly, my older sister, didn't really have to go through that, but I did," Brian asserts. When Kelly used to return home from high school social events, she would bring her mother up to date with a chat over cookies and tea. But with Brian, the tradition came to a screeching halt. His mother would wait up, an assortment of snacks spread across the kitchen table, her teapot timed perfectly with Brian's curfew. Brian, however, would grunt a good night and munch a cookie on his way to bed. "I never wanted to talk about what was going on with me," he says. "It wasn't anything personal against my mom. I didn't like that it was happening and knew that it disappointed her." Brian's unbreakable silence was the result of a mental standoff: he was attracted to the solace and curiosity his mother offered, but pressed by the need to make his life exclusively his own. Leaving her questionless and answerless in the kitchen, Brian gave his mother a hard time because he was having one as well.

Simon has been more prone to outbursts than to introversion. As his high school years began, so did his temper tantrums around his mother. When the family dinners she prepared went on too long, he would storm out without warning. When she unwittingly picked up the receiver during his phone call with a friend, his outraged hollers drove her to tears. And when she knocked politely at his bedroom to hear his thoughts on having failed a math class, he splintered the door with a hurled stereo speaker. Rising just barely above all his misbehavior, Simon, now eighteen, can make out a glimmer of its cause.

"I was acting incredibly immature, I know," he says. "But I wasn't angry at my mom all the time. I was just frustrated. I needed to clear her away. I was too close to her, that's what it honestly was. I needed to scare her, even, to get enough space to figure things out on my own." Simon was acting out with a passion that was born from his attachment. Since his love for his mom was all-encompassing, he felt he had to barge ferociously through it to move on. As he perceived his bond with his mother as too strong to loosen or ignore, he saw only one option: to explode it. Such are the backhanded tributes of many mothers' sons, featuring irreverence born from awe, and sheer spite in equal measure to love.

Teenage boys are well-known for defiance and distance, but beneath their maverick actions are emotions made known to no one. As they stride determinedly forward, they tuck away their feelings. By keeping their eyes on themselves, they keep them clear, dry, and straight ahead. Eventually, men collect like-minded acquaintances and piles of years that safely obscure their past discomfort, helping them to block out the trauma of their rush toward autonomy. But the boys who are not yet over the launches are troubled and look for cues and comfort to these other men in our midst.

Of Fathers and Flight

Along with education and inspiration, the fathers of boys provide us with an avenue away from our mothers. If it seems inevitable that dads serve as role models, however, it is also inevitable that sons are indecisive about it. From the points of view of men-in-miniature, a father is as al-luring—and inaccessible—as a son's vision of himself decades farther along. He has ties we can try on, a news-paper we can read, but a daily life we can hardly picture. Most fathers talk on the phone about "business," spend all day at "work," and come home too tired from "the job" to have clarifying talks with sons about what their routines are really like. As masters of the sort of stoicism that boys are just getting the hang of, they tend to give their sons few honest revelations. To be a man, naturally, strikes us as appealing, but so far as foreign. And our mothers seem to be split on the decision as well.

Having had to inherit, repair, and adapt to men all her life, the mother of a son finally has the chance to help cre-ate one from the ground up. But so often she stops short. Mathematically, as one of two parents, a mother deserves half the input. Ideologically, as a female in position to mold a male, she deserves the opportunity to open, broaden, and well-round us before we harden, alas, into typical men. But at some crucial point, most mothers send their sons off to father figures. I suppose that for par-ents this makes things even: mothers had their sons to themselves at the start, so fathers should get their turn as well. It makes sense for boys, too, as the older man is al-

ready up there, savvy and experienced in the rocket sci-
ence of manhood. But for mothers and sons it makes for
a widening gap.

For a while, my mother's desire to steer an even-keeled
son was visible in her efforts to keep me humble. Men
tend to get away with things, as she apparently had
learned in her twenty-eight years. Men raise their voices
and make use of their networks and hobnob their way to
great rewards and attention. My mother seemed to take
this for granted and tried to trim it around my edges. She
made me laugh at my own hairstyling attempts, let me
know when I was showing off, and warned me not to
shun or smooth-talk girls. But then, abruptly, she stopped
trimming. Her quips changed direction, urging me to
grow more robust, to strut my stuff, and join my father on
the manly side of things. She was pleased when I wore a
natty suit and tie the way he did, and scoffed when I ne-
glected to dress up. She was glad to hear my pseudo-suave
drawl as I mentioned a new girlfriend, and teased me
when I opted out of school dances. As my mother's stories of her girlhood slowed and ceased, my father stepped
up to fill their place with sports instructions, legends of
his own adolescent exploits, and a crooning outburst he
proudly called the "Singing Father Show." Simply by getting older, I seemed to have stepped over some line, into

manhood and away from my mother. Boys will be boys, and all of a sudden it was time for me to act like one, according to some clock that she held and that I could not see.

To lump sons with dads is common—but jarring, to those of us watching a mother relinquish her care. Suddenly her faith in a masculine environment seems to have overtaken her trust in our ability to choose one. Impulsively she seems to lend more importance to our gender than we do, and than she has ever done before. These are insults, but effective ones: they toughen and convince us that we must belong among men. But before they heal, the injuries are painful and private.

At nineteen, Malcolm takes offense at such male matchmaking. His father works until late at a corporate office, arriving home short of energy and temper. And despite the family friction that ensues, his mother insists on merging the two males in her house. "My dad will go off the deep end, yelling and really laying into me," says Malcolm. "And she'll sit there afterwards and tell me, *You know, he works so hard for us, and he's just tired. You know he loves you. You know it's not his fault.* And I'm like, *Come on.*" Her apologies and explanations are meant to keep her son in line behind his father; but the man's rants and raves make Malcolm only less eager to be placed there. And while his mother dissuades him from any criticism of his dad, he feels that following in that shadow would lead him far from personal goals.

"I ultimately want to be a better man than him," Malcolm says. "But she won't let me go beyond his example." Just because he is not arm-in-arm with his father doesn't mean that Malcolm is lost. However, his mother appears uneasy allowing her teenager to plot his own course.

The same categorization had been attempted on Allan for decades longer, but with hardly more success. His father was the youngest of fifteen siblings and the product of heavy-handed family discipline. Yet by applying that severity, a generation later, to the raising of his only child, the man made a foe of his son.

"There's no real affection between me and my father," Allan states, "although my mother would very much like there to be. I think that a mother naturally wants a son to respect his father first and foremost." It's a pressure Allan feels from her even now, at fifty years old, as he and his father manage to run an entertainment company together amid their frequent arguments. He continues to feel strongly for his mother, thanks to their union early on as victims of his father's aggression. But she's always felt strongly about something else. "She still wants things between me and him to be wonderful," Allan says. "I suppose she has every right to want that, but my father and I aren't likely to cross that ground—ever. My mom still thinks that a boy who respects his father will automatically be a survivor in the real world—which, by the way, ain't true. Those fathers can fuck up their sons, man."

By delivering sons onward to fathers, mothers fire themselves from their role as principal instructor. Yet in doing so, they leave their sons with one final teaching: the acceptability of mother-son separation. If a mother's willing to break her partnership with a boy, then he must be eager to follow suit—preferably so fast and thoroughly that it looks like his own idea. To swipe her inclination and make it his with haste and noise is a recognizably masculine accomplishment—his first act, in many cases, since being appointed a man. Boys fill their posts not only by behaving like adult males but by insisting that they've wanted to all along. In reality, though, we chip off the old block a tiny bit at a time, watching our mothers' reactions with virtually every small stroke.

Launched expressly in the direction of manhood, sons cannot help but look up to their dads, or at least toward them. Of course, this does not require that they mimic their fathers' lives. Growing boys see enough icons and ideas to be lured in various directions, and there is a long and distinguished history of sons' rebelling against paternal dictates. In fact, the fatherly footsteps most likely to be heeded are the ones that circle mothers. Male career choices and lifestyle decisions are not necessarily inherited, but behavior toward a mother tends to be, for a father provides a near and clear example of how a grown man is to act with his mom and vice versa. And when a mother encourages her son to join his father, she pushes him into his pattern as well.

Roy is twenty-one years old, living with his parents, and taking night classes to earn his bachelor's degree. Ambitiously, he started out opposed to imitating his father's approach to his mom. "My relationship with my mother is very, very different than Dad's, because I want it to be," he declares. "But I realize—more and more, I guess—that there may be similarities." In contrast to his hotheaded older brother and impatient father, Roy used to pride himself on being nice to his mother. Now, however, he is surprised and disappointed by his tendency to ignore her. Roy considers the matter carefully: "I don't exactly look to my father for direct cues, but I do look at how my *mother* reacts to how *he* reacts to *her*. So he hasn't exactly taught me how to treat her; ultimately, *she* has." When Roy's father comes home from work and hears from his wife about her day, he rolls his eyes at the paper, his dinner plate, or his son; but when he speaks of *his* day's events, Roy's mother listens attentively. Message received by the kid at the end of the table—over and over—and now Roy pays her less attention, too.

Among all the lessons that are passed on and dropped from father to son, this is one that's sure to stick, for it's acted out daily before our eyes. Over the course of twenty-six years, for instance, Donald has perfected the silent treatment. "Looking at my dad," he says, "what I've realized is that keeping things inside may not be commendable, but it's acceptable." Donald's mom has always been heartened by the manliness of her growing boy and pleased when he spends time with his father. So after years of witnessing his dad's early morning reserve, evening reticence, and long weekend silences, Donald finds himself following the leader—a trail that began with his mother's blessing and now leads him away from her.

"I'm withdrawn around my mom," he admits. "These days, the only time I really get in an in-depth conversation with her is if I have something specific to bring up, and it usually doesn't last long." Donald knows he could offer her more of himself; but any regret is dulled by the theory, sanctioned and proven, that men like him and his father need not open up.

A young man may be shown by older men that shutting up is permissible, but he is convinced of it by the mother who permits it. Without her consent, a son's muteness would seem stingy and rude. Even with her apparent tolerance, it does not necessarily sit well with her son. Yet as she's entrusted him to an older male trainer, he has to trust that trainer's guidance as well. It is not without discomfort, however, and that unease is what makes a son's objections sharp and his silences adamant when a mother offers him what he's no longer supposed to want: a deep, broad, and intimate discourse with the person best known for providing one.

While watching our fathers teaches us how to act around moms, it is our observations of our brothers that prompt us to shuffle secretly away from her. Through a mother's dealings with her other young men, a son is provided with a far clearer view of mother-boy manipulations than he ever could get in his own case. He notices dependencies that challenge his self-confidence. He spots causes and effects that heighten his uneasy awareness of his mother's role in his life. And such expanded outlooks often crowd sons out of tight-knit homes.

Brothers Blasting Off

Every son's mother is unique—even within the same family. My two younger brothers, for instance, have two moms who are very different from mine. Jake, now living in Moscow, has a mother who loves to play tennis and talk Russian politics, who teases him anxiously about girlfriends and secretly advises him on hair products. Luke's mom, on the other hand, takes *his* fashion advice, doesn't ask a thing about his love life, but urges reading and academics on him as fervently as she wishes true romance on Jake. And although my mother looks a lot like theirs, she acts quite differently. As a writer herself, she knows my business without having to ask for the details that my brothers are used to giving on theirs. She loves to try out old movies, new downtown restaurants, and an Italian sentence or two on the phone—all activities that are foreign to Jake, Luke, and the mothers they know. I am not likely, for that matter, to discuss girlfriends, the Kremlin, or spring fashions with mine. While Luke often feels that his mother breathes down his neck, Jake thinks of his as pretty easy-going, and I lament that mine is sometimes elusive.

Each one of my mother's sons demands a different one

of her. I have met all three of these women, and when I see them in passing they leak secrets to me about my own mom. They tip me off to things she does when I'm not around. They enlighten me on habits, policies, and attitudes of hers that she chooses not to show me. The more she worries about Jake's romantic life, the more resolved I've become not to let her loose in mine. The way she frets over Luke's academic future makes me relieved I've no interest in graduate school—and determined not to tell her if I happen to change my mind. As my mother has skillfully rotated among our triangulated looks and conversations, the members of the triangle have glimpsed, overheard, and quietly withdrawn from her.

At seventeen, Elliott is leaning away from his mother, pushed that way by her handling of his younger brother Ross. Ross's learning disabilities and explosive temper keep his mother concerned about him, and keep his older brother annoyed with her. "She asks me about his friends, his girlfriends, his grades," Elliott recounts, "and then the next night she'll start over again the second she gets me alone. She wants him to have only certain kinds of friends, who would stabilize him somehow, and to be interested in certain things—always 'for his own good,' as she says."

Elliott's growing education in mother-son management

inevitably turns his thoughts to himself and inspires questions. Things have always gone rather smoothly for Elliott; but could that be a product of his mother's frenetic smoothing when his back is turned? He's had enduring friendships and strong grades; could they have been assembled and buttressed by his mother the whole time? Chances are, of course, that his mom is no master puppeteer. Nonetheless, just to make sure, Elliott is intent on cutting the strings. "It gives me the shivers to see how involved she can get," he admits. "It just makes me want to clear out and leave her to her worrying."

To be a third-person witness to the mothering of a boy is an edgy awakening for sons. Seeing all that our mothers put into it, we become anxious to confirm that we have defined and determined our own lives. Noticing that she makes blanket statements and broad policies, we itch to shrug them off ourselves. Watching a mother tweak and refine her other young men, we become more conscious of our own workings and more eager to test the personal traits and individual skills that will motor us onward when we no longer can lean on her.

Broadening our views of our mothers usually entails removing ourselves from them—often in stealth, and occasionally in dramatic fashion. For Jeffrey, it was his mother's treatment of his older brother, Brendan, that made him eager to grow up and out of the household. His mom, an ambitious Irish Catholic immigrant, was intent on the elite and thorough education of her six children.

"All of us were born basically as fast as humans could be—nine to twelve months between us," Jeffrey says, "and we all had the same mandates from my mom: brains and schoolwork, reading and writing, get your homework done. So, increasingly, she would have something bad to say about Brendan." An aspiring actor, Brendan paid little attention to schoolwork and housework, thus bearing the brunt of his mother's exasperation. And while Brendan couldn't manage to stay on his mother's good side, Jeffrey fared much better—until suddenly, when the brothers were in their twenties, Brendan died of an aneurism.

"The effect on me was tremendous," Jeffrey says, "in terms of my mother and in terms of my life. I spent a long time trying to figure it out. What had been so wrong with my brother? Had it been Mom's pressure, the constant negative vibes and disapproval, that killed him? And if I acted the same way, would it kill me, too?" Jeffrey only half-believed in such superstition; but that half of him was sneaking away, and pulling the rest of him along swiftly.

UP AND AWAY

Could a mother fatally oppress one son, and might she be a threat to the younger one next? Having worked his way snugly into his mother's favor, would Jeffrey ever be able to wriggle completely free? These are questions that a lot of good boys put to themselves, and Jeffrey sought to answer them as soon as possible, moving across the country shortly after Brendan's death and going for long stretches—seven years, at one point—without speaking to the mother whose good side he'd up and left. Just as many sons avoid the pampering that would make them mama's boys, many others rush to escape the potent scorn that might doom them.

In order to brave the torment of wrenching away from a mother, a son must be inspired by more than her subtle and offhanded cues. And to view his mother effectively—as a multidimensional person, from several angles, and from a clarifying distance—a son needs more than just his own two eyes. Other male members of the family may give us various and crucial signals about mothers, men, and the lines to be drawn between them. But what they do not give us is comfort as we attempt to draw those lines and move into our own territories. Male role models help to spring boys from their mothers' sides, but that action provides neither escape nor release: instead, it's a severance that hurts. Assurance and reassurance were their mothers' forte, and sons must go painfully without them as they join their fathers and brothers in a manly flight from contentment.

Liftoff

Years ago, our mothers began our countdown to independence with their bright talk of our strengths and futures. But it's up to boys to count up, and they do so loudly and forcefully. We keep meticulous record of our heights and weightlifting abilities, our batting averages and math grades. Young men keep track of how many beers they can drink, how many girlfriends they've had, the costs of their fantasy cars, the sizes of their fathers' salaries. Even our sexual educations are measured in a numerical system of "bases," as if fledgling relations with women were countable and even winnable. Sons are made mathematicians by their craving for ascension: calculating, drawing, and eagerly completing the steps toward far-off adulthood as the liftoff from their mothers trembles in their heads. And the moment they actually leave home, it thunders.

To a boy who spent his childhood ticking off tiny

achievements, getting into college seemed to me a celebratory end to all the bean counting. After years of crossing blurry lines and arguing for advancement, this was a resounding feat: a public graduation amid pomp and a circus of festivities. In the week or two before my departure, my mother helped me pile socks, choose posters, and feel the full-body tingle of a momentous occasion. Together, she and I figured out how many sweatshirts and what size laundry basket I'd need; but as soon as I got to college, she could no longer help me with my fervent accounting. Although my first anxious breakaway was behind me, another graduation had entered my sights: dangling there after thirty-odd class credits and four progressive years; begging to be reeled in one calculation at a time—and without the aid of my mother.

Men are sent off by mothers on missions that are strictly solo. Their mothers' lifelong assistance is not forgotten; but it must be surpassed, as boys are expected to advance into college, jobs, and their own lives under their own power. To work toward full male autonomy, we must do without the woman who's always supported us; and the pain that comes with that separation sparks us onward. To disengage from our little boyhoods, we must put mileage between us and the person who loomed largest back then; and our agitation as we do so only proves that it's necessary. Ultimately, to distinguish our own precious thrust and momentum, we must leave hers behind. And we do this by discounting her expertise and detaching from her emotions.

There was a time when our mothers could interpret our various moods and respond expertly. This is precisely the stage we must jettison to move on. As baby boys, we were somewhat open books: pouting could be read as sadness, bubbling smiles as the opposite; bawling and grinning told our stories all day long. It is no coincidence that our emotions and identities have become more cryptic; it is a conscious achievement of sons. We have banged shut as we've grown, walling off our mothers from compre-hension—and we have done so on purpose. To dumb-found the person who once knew more about us than we did says that we've come a long way.

Frankly, I was pleased that my mother was not a fan of the oddball rock and reggae bands that I played as loud as my secondhand stereo system would go. After all, rock 'n' roll was founded on its famous ability to shock the old folks; without a mother's raised eyebrows or covered ears, a son's cutting-edge sound lacks sharpness. So when I came home from college one weekend with a lively sam-pling of what I'll call Coastal Folk, or White Carribean, I was mortified by her response. *"Jimmy Buffet?"* she gasped, pointing at the cassette player and keeping time with her sneaker. "That's who this is? I used to *love* Jimmy Buffet!" It was my turn to be shocked, as she jogged into the living room to look for something. Indeed, buried between other records on a forgotten shelf of music was her own yellowed album by an ungrayed Jim, which she held high in victory. And it was on that shelf, to my dismay, that my brand-new collection was soon stored as well.

To be offbeat is to make certain that we're banging our own drums. "I'm the enigma," says Rick, with pride. "My older brothers were easier for my mom to grasp. They did well in college, played sports that she came and watched, and visited home all the time. But with me she's like, *What on earth is going on with Rick?* " Undeniably, Rick has changed since he's been at college. He is much happier playing loud music on his Walkman and avoiding chats after weekend family dinners than his mother ever knew him to be. He talks with her only every so often; but he speaks to me, with firm pleasure, of his graduation from predictability. "I always seem to be changing, and I'm moody," he admits. "It's hard for my mom to get her hands on me, and I don't tell her enough to give her much of a picture of my life now. So she still thinks of me as this quiet, passive kid. And when I get mad or suddenly want to play the guitar or study a religion or something, she finds it upsetting." Rick, on the other hand, finds it encouraging. To revolve and drift is a sure sign that a son has gained his own space. To have expanded in various directions is to have grown as a man. And if such jagged expansion doesn't sit well with a mother, then that's all the more proof that he has distinguished himself from her.

In our days of cribs and crawling, our mothers' emotions played as important a role as their wisdom. Thus, according to sons' law of inverses, these emotions also must be disregarded in order to quicken and confirm our rise from immaturity.

On André's first day of college, for instance, he was surprised to find something on his desk barely an hour after his mom had dropped him off—and vexed when he realized that it was a long, personal letter describing her feelings about leaving him there. As an only child, André had always felt close to his mother. At that moment, however, his reaction was to hustle in the opposite direction. "I was a bit weirded out by it, to be honest. I just didn't have room for her sentiments right then," he says. "I mean, I was a college freshman about to start my first week; I had enough to think about." Amid a stampede of new acquaintances and a carnival of classes and events, André felt overloaded. Higher education, as his mother had reiterated often, is about high-speed action and high-stakes ambition, not about mulling over all the internal conflicts involved. "It was good that she let me in on her emotions, it really was," says André. "But I didn't know how to respond." Therefore, he never did. Too busy looking forward to school at the time, as his mother had urged, he was unable to take an in-depth look at the sentiments of either mother or son.

Along with his own mixed feelings, André was disturbed by the mixed message often received from a mother. To be a successful man, she choruses with the rest of our world, a son must prioritize his masculine development over all else. And so he does—in spite of her contradictory desire to be closely included. Stepping away from maternal strengths, such as her omniscience and her emotions, he focuses stringently on his own powers of advancement. It's no wonder that independent young men avoid substantial dealings with their mothers: they've been instructed that, like all other distractions and indulgences, they could hold them back, even drag them down. Nothing is to be paid as much attention as wherever a young man is headed, not even the woman who first taught him precisely that.

Ground Control

I could have called home. Of course, it was rural west Africa, not exactly a hub of modern telecommunications; and I was an adult, technically, having finished my first year of college. But it wouldn't have been impossible to find a phone, just once during those two months, to let my mother know I was okay. I'd gone to help construct a health clinic, to spend a summer with people I didn't know about—beginning with myself. I was taking few showers, rickety cross-country buses in the middle of the night, inevitable and evitable risks. I was throwing myself out there, often scared and alone; which was precisely what kept me from calling my mom. To spend that scratchy phone call paying heed to her expertise and feelings would have halted my progress. But more than that, to get in touch simply seemed unneccessary. As I was testing all she'd ever taught me about ambition and initiative, toughness and heart, she was already along for the whole bumpy ride. It hardly occurred to me that she could feel left out. Automatically and permanently, she was with me whether she knew it or not.

Sons who leave home are suddenly distant. We hold ourselves at arm's length with a sense of conviction that may seem peculiar, but isn't. If a son seems unwilling to make any efforts to include his mom, it's simply because he knows that she is already ingrained in his ongoing life. It's a relief, as he tries to connect with an ever wider range of people, to carry a deep and mobile connection to the person at the heart of where he's from. It's a comfort, as he heads out to make himself known, to have one person who's known him from his very beginnings. And it's in awkward deference to her prominent place within him that he resists his mother's attempts to gain further entrance.

"She's with you no matter what," says Julian. "That's what my mother can't seem to understand. My dad is always like, *Yes, my son, go on. I trust your judgment because I gave it to you. My blood runs through your veins. Call when you feel like it.* But my mother seems to think that in terms of her, it's out of sight, out of mind." Even as a teenager, Julian used to talk to his mother for hours on end. Now, in his second year of graduate school, he admits to calling her infrequently and to getting annoyed when she complains of it. But Julian's irritation is not caused by his mother's attempts to enter his current life as much as by her inability to trust that she's already in it.

"Her voice is in my head," he explains. "As I make all

these decisions every day, I can hear in my mind what my mother would say. As I go around meeting people, I always consider what she'd think of them. I don't live my life according to her opinions; I have plenty of my own. But I do have her feelings inside me." These exist in the makeup of every man, whether he chooses to admit it or not.

While much attention is commonly paid to the link between fathers and sons, this often amounts—as crucial and memorable as it is—to in-flight guidance. It's a mother who provides the launching pad, boost, and open communication the whole while, and it's her voice that whispers in her son's head long after he's left her arms and home base. Heroically and unceremoniously, a mother serves as ground control her son's entire life. Therefore, hearing mothers fret over the recent quality of the connection, most sons have trouble seeing the crisis.

Geoff is busy with his engineering job, tired of living in a cramped apartment with four guys, and sorry that his conversations with his mother are so few and far between. "The truth is that I think of her all the time," he tells me. "And the other truth is that it's really *hard* not to talk to her. At first, when I moved out of home, there were all these times that I wanted to pick up the phone and spill my guts to her. But that's not what's supposed to happen.

That's not what living in your own place is about. And gradually I've gotten better at being completely independent." This was the direction in which Geoff's mother had pointed him as a little boy: solid job, swarms of friends, capable independence. So to maintain that status, Geoff takes care to stay within the bounds of his hard-earned space. "She might not admit it," he says, "but I know she'd be dismayed if I called home every three minutes, crying about how hard they make me work and how hectic my big, bad life is." Geoff is at the point now that both he and his mother worked for, year in and year out. And though it's not as scintillating as either of them might have hoped, he must continue to make the best of it and the best of himself, on his own.

I know his resolve firsthand. When things fall apart, I tend not to. Instead, I clamp into a mute toughness which I have certainly picked up from my mom. I can count the times I've seen her cry; I can almost put a number on the tears themselves. And I certainly remember all the times she didn't: when she stabbed herself in the hand with a pair of scissors, requiring dozens of stitches; when our family dog died, leaving the rest of us dissolved. When she does break down, it's literally that. Her face crashes into itself, her voice halts completely, bangs of hair close her off, and everything stops as if gone terribly awry. In fear of this quiet calamity, I watched my mother bustle about my new dorm room the day she brought me to college. She straightened things unnecessarily, arranged my new comforter on my new bed three different ways until it was time to leave me there. And then she left. Her mouth was stiff as she said good-bye, but nothing more or less as she led my father out the door.

It wasn't until I finished college that my dad gave me the whole story like a graduation present: An hour or so into the drive home, my mother was at the wheel in silence. As they passed back into Connecticut, some slow, corny pop song came on—although I could have sworn she listened only to classical—and she burst into loud sobs, losing control, pulling off the road, and sitting there and sobbing harder. When my father told me, I found it hard to picture. More than that, I thought that she was wrong. By going off, I was going nowhere that would take me from her. While I was opening up my life to all sorts of new people and ideas, her presence and beliefs were not being ousted. On the contrary: I was making more of the life my mother gave me with her very much in mind. I suppose that she'd say she was simply lamenting the passage of time, the irretrievability of things—but what do time and things matter in the face of our stretching, growing, unbreakable friendship?

I have never discussed this with my mother, however. It is one of the conversations that I've felt far too harried to have. She has never told me that she cried that day. And I have not yet told her that she needn't have.

A boy is a rocket man, of course, only in his own mind. His launch, as climactic as it feels, is actually common to all children and inevitable as he grows toward independence. Moreover, he does not leave his mother beneath him, as his connection to her—his ground control—is never severed. Although it's sometimes jumbled, occasionally disregarded, and most often soundless, contact with our mothers is as active and vital a piece of equipment as anything we take with us from home.

CHAPTER THREE

INSIDE OUT

Does all that time I spent with my son, the right-from-wrong and all that, mean anything to him now that he lives on his own? These days he certainly isn't as eager to please me as he once was. Does he care about that less than he used to?

HAVING SPENT MONTHS INTERROGATING MEN OF all ages in a variety of settings and states, it was time for me to hear from their mothers. So I bought my first modem and rode it onto the information superhighway. Fast-moving cybermoms were everywhere, from chat rooms on diaper rash to Web pages on Wild Wilderness Weekends for Women, and for months they told me about their sons. They offered their memories, confessions, and concerns, and when I asked for them, they gave me their questions.

What place do I have in his thinking these days, now that he is gone from home? I know that mothers

must let go. But how much? From his point of view,
must he put his mother completely aside for now?

Responses from young men may be startling when we reconsider our attitudes and at last—in anonymity—turn ourselves inside out. Our mothers are very much on our minds, despite our frequent behavior to the contrary. Their roles in our present goings-on and future ambitions grow as we do, long after our declarations of independence. In the privacy of our heads, we incorporate our mothers in our business, acting detachedly while feeling closely linked.

Our secrecy on this front may be extreme, but it is not outrageous; nor is it that different from the behavior of our mothers. Like us, they try, with mixed success, not to unload their inevitable moods and misgivings as we depart for adulthood. Striking out on our own, we stifle our emotions for the same reason our mothers do: to ensure no delay or sidetracking of our personal progress. But the parallel does not end there. What we keep from our mothers, and even hide from ourselves, is a mirror that flashes and reflects our mothers' sentiments. As boys become men, they suffer through the same emotional roller coaster as their mothers.

Dancing in that mirror are five distinct feelings that

may be familiar, although common knowledge has it that they belong to someone else.

First, just as our mothers can be wounded by our foul-ups as boys, we feel so bonded to our moms that their blunders become ours.

Second, we go through a crisis of sorts when we flee our mothers' domains: a sense of loss and a reversal of the laws of behavior that complement the more famous syndrome of the mothers who watch us leave.

Third, we crave our mothers' approval in the same way they seek ours: covertly, uncomfortably, and increasingly as we become adult acquaintances.

Fourth, a growing boy has a deep-seated desire to protect his mother, as she sought to protect him, from the harm that looms in the wide world.

Fifth, we feel as obligated to our mothers, and as grateful for our time together, as they feel toward us—although we keep this emotion, like the other four, more private than she.

Such attitudes are not publicized, since according to lore they are more maternal than masculine. But as sons embark on adulthood, we are wrenched by all five of these feelings in moments we keep to ourselves.

Double Trouble

My son has certainly gone through his rebellious times, times when I thought, "Oh, God, now he's acting like a real boy." And it's hard not to feel like those reflect on me as his mother. They make me wonder if I've taught him well or enough. When he acts out, I can't help but take it personally. I can't just let his mistakes go, because they feel like they might be my mistakes too.

Getting in trouble has been lamented and cheered as an international male pastime through the ages. Black-suited bad guys, swashbucklers, and scoundrels are immortalized in every medium known to man. Rare is the macho rock star who bellows about how good it is to be good. Rarer still are popular books and TV shows about perfectly well-behaved young men. In the course of male development, *adolescent* has become synonymous with troublesome, *teenage* with rebellious, *college-age* with reckless. Mischief and mishaps seem to come naturally to boys; but the trouble is not theirs alone. Rushing into the vast arena of manhood, many sons trip and fall over themselves; and when they do, they bring their mothers

THE SECRET LOVE OF SONS

down with them. Although it's a linkage that's resisted and griped about by sons, their tumbles and stunts are not exclusively theirs.

As a well-mannered little boy, I never would have considered getting a tattoo. But in my twenties, with my options wide open, I couldn't wait. As men, we can do what we want, where we want, in whatever shape and color we see fit. I suppose I was reveling in that lawlessness—or, more likely, testing it out—when I entered the Ancient Art Tattoo Parlor in Roanoke, Virginia. Seeing the thing on my arm months later, my mom gasped, "What were you *thinking?*" But for any man who performs unruly acts, whether grave or frivolous, it is not a matter of thinking. I had no theory to present, no sober credo that could explain the rashness of the action. My mother's shock seemed to me to come from afar: from the maternal realm of clear and cautious programming that I had exited, on cue, when I entered adulthood.

But my mother was not far away. On the contrary: she was right with me, so close by that I'd apparently branded her arm with mine. Judging by her discomfort, my new look was her new look, for better or worse. In the midst of my random constellations of freckles and scars, I had intended to found a bright blue star of my own, and I did. But it was her mark too, a five-pointed flaw that she would have to live with. I had wanted to claim myself in the daring way that other American rocket men claimed the moon: by stabbing something in that would flag my ownership. She, however, had a stake in me as well. What I accomplished that day, egged on by legal adulthood and masculine bravado, was not exactly what I'd planned. For the hell of it and for other manly reasons, I had gone and given my mom a tattoo.

Tom, another troublemaker, rediscovered the same bond with his mother and also tried to shrug it off. "For the longest time," he recalls, "she thought I was a little angel—until finally the truth struck, once I was out on the loose." Tom and his best friend had shared a secret history of minor troublemaking, but when they visited a nearby ski lodge and stole two duffle bags—full, it turned out, of the resort manager's belongings—the secret was out. "It was more of a prank than anything else," Tom says, "but we got busted and it just snowballed. My mom couldn't believe it when I told her about the police. She almost broke down there and then." If she was upset at that news, she was floored by the next: Not more than three weeks after the ski lodge incident, Tom was arrested in town for blowing up a half-dozen mailboxes with explosives. Before and after he was arraigned in court, his mother wept openly and asked him repeatedly *why*. But there was no motive to speak of, only Tom's vague urge to act radically and his contention that it had nothing to do with her. "I felt bad about it, real bad for her," he says, "but that's the kind of mischief that a guy gets into, I guess. Anyway, she didn't do anything wrong, I did. It shouldn't have been her problem." Yet it was clear from her tears and questions that it was.

Mothers insist that our misbehavior is theirs. Whether we live upstairs or miles away, they wince at our short-comings and panic when we go off the deep end. Men have scrawled thick, angry books on the dangers of such a smothering alliance. Popular comedies and tragedies are brimming with moms who are overbearing and overreactive to their sons' misadventures. But what few men admit is what all of us feel: that very same inextricable link to a mother's behavior. Just as she is invested in all that her son does and does wrong, he implicates himself in her mistakes—and gets angry when she condemns the both of them.

When mothers tell bad jokes or wear ugly sweaters, we are as horrified as if they were tattooed on our arms. Should they mispronounce names or misinterpret stories, you'd think they'd put dynamite in our mailboxes. For sons taking their first breaths of independence, a mother's slightest misbehavior feels suffocating. As we try not to rock our own boats, our mothers' least missteps make us feel wobbly. But it is we who pull our moms onboard and then find them close enough to suffocate us. Without telling anyone, sons equate our mothers' fates and mistakes with our own.

Although my mother has a range of titles and is many different things to many different people, it would be hard to call her a hindrance. She's stylish and attractive, her clothes casually up-to-date, her hair chic when it has to be, a winning tumble when it doesn't. She's impressive: accomplished journalist and multilingual conversationalist, black-belt weed-whacker and gourmet cook. She tells engaging stories, makes quick and accurate debate points, likes sports, and enjoys the sorts of movies that I do—without laughing too hard or exclaiming out loud. Hardly a liability, she was unmockable even by my ruthless schoolmates, admirable even by me. But when she took charge of a surprise party for my high school graduation, she was simply and awfully my mother—and there was no more prominent post she could descend to.

Too many balloons, I thought, glancing around once the hooting and singing had died down. The yard looked like Romper Room. And the technicolor paper plates and cups and (*no, please*) festive hats had to be her touch as well, with all the panache of a six-year-old's piñata party. I was nearly twenty—was that a *volleyball* net? Did she expect my college-minded crowd to frolic in the grass for hours of setting, spiking, and sweating through their collared shirts and blouses? My mother toured the party gingerly, a china shop among bulls, trying her best. I kept a wincing eye on her as she pushed the hors d'oeuvres (*quiche? for the football captain?*) and offered around nonalcoholic beer (*kill me now*). As I saw it, my mother did everything she could to make the party a big success and to keep me from being one. With each stylistic blunder, she took me down a peg. As she shot the breeze with the crowd I'd wanted to impress, she threatened to shoot me down for good—although no one else seemed to be watching her as closely, distracted, perhaps, by the volleyball game in progress. I was flying the coop, off to college, free from my family—and so closely and perilously linked to my mom that I could hardly breathe.

Such scenes could star only a mother and could agonize only her son. But why are they so universal? Jim provides a few clues: "I can't help thinking, *Jeez, c'mon, Mom. Help me out here a little bit,*" he says. "She embarrasses me all the time, but it's only in front of other people, and I'm sure I notice more than anyone else." For a man on his own, making friends is akin to making progress. So when Jim brought home his college roommate for the first time, his life's advancement was on the line. And when his mother began to chat about her new passion for computers and the friends she'd met on-line, Jim felt jeopardized. "My roomate asked politely, *So what are you doing today, Mrs. Kimball?*" he remembers. "And she started talking about this mystery woman she'd been E-mailing back and forth with and the fact that she was planning to go meet her and on and on about her infatuation with computers. And I was sitting there thinking, *This is so humiliating.* I mean, it sounded like we were on *Oprah:* 'Mothers Who Meet Mothers On-Line.'"

In retrospect, Jim realizes that he was alone in his horror. "I don't think my roommate even cared," he says. "He may have even thought it was cool. Who knows? But at the time I was like, *My mother is a lunatic.* And that made me feel like a failure."

A son reacts twice as harshly toward his mother as situations would seem to dictate, and that's because she is behaving for the both of them. Although he's in his forties, Jacob still feels that every time his mother exposes herself, he is bared to the public as well. "She hasn't had a great education," he explains, "but she is extremely well-read and an avid listener. So she tends to present herself as an authority on whatever subject happens to be talked about at the time. Even when she's around people who are actual authorities, who *do* have expertise, my mom starts pretending like she has more of it and takes over the conversation." At a recent dinner party with some new acquaintances, Jacob's mother—born and bred in America's heartland—began to lecture the group on the history of the British royal family. Her son, meanwhile, felt like hiding under the table. "Her know-it-all shtick is just painful for me," he says. "It's so glaringly obvious that she ends up making a fool of herself and a fool of me. I'm left just squirming in my seat." Jacob's repulsion from his mother, naturally, is caused by his attachment to her. "You're linked to your mom," he says, "whether you want to be or not. That's the real truth." And on certain occasions, the link can be a true problem.

Sons, as a rule, don't cut mothers much slack. We keep a tighter rein on her activities and conversations around us than anyone else's, act even less tolerant and more suspicious of her indiscretions than our own. We holler at her to loosen up, to stop living our lives, to let us be us; meanwhile, we flout those very orders in our zealous reactions to our mothers. A son gives his mother a million instructions, but he would never give the reason for them—that he perceives himself through perceptions of her, just as she's always done with him.

The Prelife Crisis

*It was hard when he left for college. There's a sense,
as a mother without your son around, that you're not
quite sure what to do with yourself, or how to be "good"
anymore. I was a good mother, and suddenly I was supposed to be good at just being a woman again, without him. It was a difficult transition. It was hard to
know how to feel about myself for a while.*

This confession is echoed and upheld around the
world. In books, articles, and my own interviews, people
are quick to theorize on mothers' midlife crises and
empty-nest syndromes. Critical summaries abound on
the confusion that must set in with the loss of maternal
roles and duties. But almost nobody acknowledges that
men have prelife crises of their own. Good sons, like good
mothers, are discombobulated at the onset of their independence: there is no rule book to replace the one that
expires with their childhoods.

In the back of a coffee shop, the interviewee across the
table is wrapping up our discussion of the mandates of
manhood. "Everyone is telling you to be aggressive here,"

he says, "and that can be disconcerting. Everyone expects you to 'Take a job' and 'Seize the future' and 'Find yourself a good woman' all of a sudden. But that sort of assertiveness would not have gone over well when we were seven."

I agree: "That was precisely how you'd be annoying and get spanked."

"That's right. That's exactly right," he says. "So you feel like you're being *bad*, in your mother's book, when you're just being assertive—"

"Sorry," comes a voice from the table next to us. We both turn to see a man in his early thirties. "I'm sorry to interrupt, but I was overhearing your conversation," he says, "and you guys are *so* right on."

"Really?" I ask.

"God, yes," the man says.

"That's funny," my tablemate mumbles. I wonder if he is embarrassed—or suspicious, rather, that I'd prearranged the scene, tape recorder and all.

"I mean, I'm just sitting over there," our visitor goes on, "and I'm like, *Hey, those guys are going through just what I'm going through.*" He laughs, hair bobbing. "I was like, *Man, I was confused about my mom. I didn't know how to act around her either.* Totally like you were saying just now, about still wanting to be a good boy."

"And that sounds right to you?" I ask.

"Totally, totally. But it's not like you're ever going to talk about it, right?" He laughs and takes a step nearer, closing our triangle. Folding his arms, he asks me, "So, were you the oldest?"

To be honest, such spontaneous support groups are rare. However, potential members are everywhere, as grown sons are operating without instructions. When we are little, our assignment is clear. The rules are simply and repeatedly stated. Bad boys shake things up. They are too aggressive, stay out too late, talk too loudly. They attract attention from the adult world of librarians, friends' parents, and school principals. They take things that don't belong to them, raise their voices, make scenes—and by doing so, lose the favor of their mothers. Good boys, on the other hand, refrain. They are to act conscientious and spend time quietly around the house, pleasing their moms and themselves in the process.

But then the rules are reversed. The moment we graduate from home, a mother's handbook of restraint is to be thrown out. She provided the ideals that steered us safely to good boyhood; now, we must not only disregard those mantras but disobey them to be good men. Men find success by acting out, grabbing attention, avoiding old habits of avoidance. Real men make a splash, some noise, and names for themselves—the way a real teenager would get in trouble with his mom. Moms used to be wary of loud, male hyperactivity, but the second sons stop being kids, that's exactly how to make it big. And this sweeping rule reversal leaves many sons baffled as to how to include their mothers once they've left their childhoods behind.

Leaving home, we step into all sorts of manly training regimes, but into a void when it comes to our mothers. Male elders take us under their wings and stress the need to impress older males. Younger females teach us, through various means, about attracting young women. But we are no longer instructed with respect to our moms, and that sudden drop-off is disorienting. To behave, in our boyhoods, was to keep a hold on ourselves and go easy around our mothers. But manhood is no-holds-barred, full-steam ahead, and away from all that was easy. So how can we incorporate the author of the virtuous guidebook that we've been told to toss aside?

Surrounded by four loud and overathletic housemates, my mother seemed occasionally entertained but more often anxious. My brothers and I had a habit of picking up any object, round or square, hard or soft, precious or produce, and throwing it at one another. Fresh avocados and antique ashtrays zipped across the kitchen; dog bones and staplers were always airborne. We invented baseball games in the car, ran football plays around the dining room table, played three-man hockey with frozen hamburger patties on the just-washed floor. My father often joined in, winging a book or hard-boiled egg at one of us and then shrugging helplessly at his wife. And watching my mom duck and sigh, I got the sense we were a bit too much. She wanted us to cut it out, tone it down, just sit still. So I worked to tame the hectic masculine energy that crackled through me and threatened her bulging house and patience.

When I left home for college, however, my mother began to pump up that frenetic boyishness rather than tamp it down. What worried her now, more than anything, was inactivity. Was I having enough fun, letting loose as I should? Why wasn't I going to the spring formal, trying out for baseball—hell, even having a keg party if I saw fit? Back home, our circus-style energy made all three of us a hazard; but in the worldwide race of all-around guys, it served as our protection and our promise. My mother was eager to hear my accounts of fast and furious weekends, and would have been pleased at my throwing around footballs and vacation ideas and rooming arrangements. But never having celebrated such rowdiness with my mom, I wasn't prepared to start now. The boyish zeal that used to leave her flinching and exhausted was suddenly in high demand, and I was struck dumb by that contrast.

Men advance in life by talking to strangers, biting off more than we can chew, and refusing to keep their hands to themselves. As such aggressive pursuits take over their daily lives, they often exclude the women who once prohibited them.

When Cory was young, his mother admonished him for his overactivity, and with good reason: he broke furniture, shattered household rules, yelled, cursed, and shook off all authority. "I was a wild one," Cory admits. "My mother really had her hands full with me, all the time. I must have been a nightmare." But when he entered the job force not long ago, to Cory's surprise and pleasure, those qualities suddenly worked to his advantage. "That's the way men act in banking." He laughs. "And in a lot of heavy-duty jobs. I see it every day." His supervisor throws tantrums. His successful colleagues become more successful by bending and breaking conventional rules. At Cory's firm, and wherever men make deals and money, their willingness to barrel forward is what gets them places—and what leaves their mothers out of the loop.

"It's just hard to picture telling my mom, *Yeah, I really*

kicked ass on this account! Or: *So, Mom, guess what. I demanded the money, scared it out of them, and now it's mine!*" Cory says. "Even though I was never quite able to be a calm, sweet little kid, that's what she always wanted. And now that that's not demanded of me, I feel awkward saying to her, *Hey, look what I can get away with, now that I don't have to obey you!* So I just tell her that work's fine these days. You know: *Fine, Mom. Uh-huh. Not bad. Fine.*"

Now that Darren is in his thirties and has gotten the hang of it, he can admit that he was a bit bewildered a decade ago when he left the context that his mother had provided. "One thing she used to tell me repeatedly, and that really stuck in my mind," he says, "is that what she wanted more than anything else for me and my brother was that we would be good people. To be 'good' had profound meaning for her." It's sage encouragement; but when Darren's collision with manhood tossed the meaning of that adjective up in the air, it left him baffled. "For me, there was a lot of confusion between this goodness that she talked about and being ambitious," he reflects. "I think that once I left home, I heaped a lot of stuff under the umbrella of what might not be good in her eyes. Lust is not good. Having sex is not good. God knows, masturbating would be bad. But the truth is that, as a man, you're going to do all those things. Even being too ambitious might not be good, because it's associated with being too masculine and too testosterone-driven—and that never pleased her before."

After living and working on his own for more than a decade, Darren's become accustomed to the ideological upheaval. "Now I've cleared up some of that," he says. "I'm more comfortable being manly and ambitious than I was when I was younger, I think. But that was a real dilemma, and there's nobody you want to talk to about it."

The dilemma, of course, can be exciting. Sons who are released from childhood rules are often giddy with the freedom of being turned out of the gate. However, we are paralyzed when it comes to approaching our mothers. After learning to disregard maternal laws, why would we still request and obey our moms' verdicts? Once we've been notified that a mother's home guidebook has expired, how can we trust her opinions on current events? Our instinct is to seek her out—and therein lies our crisis. Stretched between the vague pull of individualism and the familiar appeal of their mothers, young men are pained and silenced by the tension.

A Mother's Nod

I do feel, a lot of the time, that I'm on trial in front of him. I care about what he thinks of me, not only as his mother but as a person and as a woman. I want him to respect me, especially now that he's adult. I think he's grown into a good person, and I hope that he believes the same thing about me.

As they grow up and spread out, sons are not only lone voyagers but ambassadors, representing to the world how well a mother raised her man. To some onlookers, a man's dirty socks and shoddy bathroom habits suggest a maternal deficiency. To others, thin skin and spoiled manners could mean she overdid it. No matter what, to be labeled a mama's boy condemns mama and boy alike, and to be famously successful brings applause for both. But to a son, just as important as any public jury is the singular verdict of a mother herself. As she would appreciate his general approval, so he finds himself coveting hers—but not saying so. Instead, anxious to satisfy both of them, he simply demonstrates to her that he's turned out well. Adult men are to conduct their affairs according to their own opinions. Therefore, it is in silence that we seek our mothers' approval, and in secret that the approval resonates.

I was more nervous than I let on, after inviting my mom to see my new apartment. My girlfriend and I had painted the walls a delicate cream color that suddenly, a few minutes before her arrival, blared ghastly yellow. ("She'll think it's funky," my girlfriend assured me. "It's *banana*," I insisted. "And it doesn't matter what she thinks.") The buzzer rang and my mother showed up with flowers, even though I had nothing resembling a vase, and with a bottle of wine, which sent us on a semisuccessful hunt for glasses. ("These are fine," I whispered to my girlfriend, coming up with Dixie cups the size of shot glasses. "Who cares, anyway?") My mom was tired from a full day spent crisscrossing the city, and could have used a chair. Instead we sat on the bare kitchen floor, looking out on my empty living room and the full, laundry-strewn tenement building a few feet from my window. I scrutinized her face as she sipped from her tiny cup, discussed bedroom setups, and brainstormed on curtains. "I think the place is terrific," she pronounced at last. "And these walls," she said, "are truly . . . funky." I took her word for it and we toasted a couple of times, crumpling our cups. Believing her made me believe in myself, and with her smiling support the place felt like a home.

Like me, many sons seem unlikely and unwilling to pander to a mother's opinion. Kenneth, for instance, would hardly speak to his mom once he was old enough to decide not to. She had left his father after her scandalous affair with a priest, whereupon Kenneth had gone to live with his dad and brothers and ultimately settled in a different state. All along, he shirked her attempts to catch up.

"I insisted that she act hands-off as I grew older," Kenneth affirms. "Especially as I was going into my adult life, I could never stand any of her interference. I had never had that nurturing, and I certainly didn't want it now that I was on my own." As a result, any maternal attempts to guide or advise Kenneth were met with solid resistance. "I've had no time for that," he says. "I've always been like, *Don't even try it. You gave up on that when you left us. Let me do my thing.*"

Kenneth, however, has always been aware of his mother's high expectations for him. And lately he's sought to confirm that they've been met. Now in his forties, he is proud to be the owner of a popular restaurant: so pleased, in fact, that he's invited his mother several times to come eat—on the house—and see things for herself. "I think she definitely takes pride in what I've managed to do in this city," he says. "When she comes down, she can see that there's a nice clientele and that business is thriving. A restaurateur has kind of a public lifestyle, and I'm out in front with the customers and the public all the time and I think that's what pleases her most. She had a hand in teaching me, way back when, to get along with people in the world, and seeing it in action seems to do her good." Not only do these visits gladden his mother, they also make Kenneth feel complete. After years of ex-communication, he has let her in on his life's accomplishments in the hope of feeling more accomplished. And after a few brief visits and unprecedented talks, Kenneth has satisfied both of their hopes. "She knows who I am these days," he says. "And I have to admit, it makes me feel good that after all these years, she's proud of me."

Like Kenneth, Steve describes his relationship with his mother as never having been particularly close. The oldest of three children, he used to fight with her about his social life and spend far more time with his father, who served as his athletic coach and his mentor. Then Steve left to attend technical college, found a job, and hardly looked back. Yet when he recently decided to switch coasts, he brought his mother along for the weeklong moving trip.

"It was her idea," Steve says, "so that I wouldn't have to do the entire cross-country drive by myself. But I didn't hesitate to accept. I'm fond of telling my friends that it was scary: I mean, I hadn't spent that much time with my mom since early high school. But I think it was a good thing." It was a chance for Steve to open up his new life to her, after fifteen years of leading it in private. And therefore, to his surprise, it was a pleasure. "She got to see me go through some decision-making processes, in setting up a place and arranging a life, which she hadn't ever seen before. And that made me feel better about how I was doing." Despite all his previous solo ventures, Steve did not feel truly accomplished until his mother saw him as so.

A son's need for a mother's endorsement is often painful, however, twisting us toward her and then snapping us back away. Dave, for instance, went so far as to pretend he isn't gay. Dave is his mother's only child, and has shared a close relationship with his mom all his life, although she vehemently disapproved of his homosexuality well into his adulthood. "She lamented that I'd never be able to walk into a big party with a woman on my arm," he says. "She quite desperately wanted me to be a success, but a success on her terms. And her terms included marriage, children, and a straight and impressive lifestyle." As her dismay continued, it cut deeper. "It certainly entered my thinking," Dave says, "in that I felt like a failure and a coward a lot of the time. I would listen to her complaints and feel like a disappointment."

Although he has become a highly successful artist and has gone to plenty of big parties with plenty of people on his arm, Dave never numbed to his mother's rebukes. Finally, as she lay fatally ill, he made a startling concession: he got engaged to be married to a woman. "It was only as a gift for my mother," he reflects. "I deeply wanted to give her something major and get her blessing in return, even though I pretty much knew it was all hogwash." The half-hearted engagement was dissolved just after Dave's mother died; but for a handful of days, he basked in her happiness with his life.

"It was a wonderful feeling—although, naturally, I feel very odd about the arrangement in retrospect," he says. "It was all an act, and one shouldn't have to act in front of one's mother. That's sad. And it makes me rather sad. But at the time, it was like giving her the biggest diamond that I could afford"—a diamond that reflected well, if artificially, on both mother and son.

Few of us would go to such lengths, and few of us are expected to. Men are meant to lead their own lives, not contort them to meet maternal directions. I have not lived my life in a straight line, guided and embraced by my mother's smiles and nods. I have had relationships, jobs, and misadventures that have made her shudder. I have cultivated theories, whims, and attitudes that brashly oppose hers. I am hammering together my own life according to my own blueprints, as the masculine master plan says I must. But when the labor and noise of construction die down, I want my mother to join me at my site, step inside, and be impressed. Like other men, I have not watched and obeyed her reactions all along, but rather hope that she will watch me and my actions with pride. Only the woman who observed him at his very beginnings could provide the closure that a man desires.

To gain a mother's esteem is a goal that burns just as fiercely as any other manly ambition, although it's far less publicly celebrated. Sons' need to reconnect with their mothers is buried below the surface of bold young men on their self-serving way; but it kindles inside them, spreading undetected.

Manning Our Mothers

I certainly had the sense that I had to protect my son from all he might face as a man in the world today. There is so much out there that threatens males in our society, so much bad that they can fall into. I remember looking at him when he was little and saying, "You don't even know what's in store for you," and wanting to just keep him there, safe and sound, away from it all, and knowing at the same time that I couldn't.

"Your mama's so old, she coughs dust."

"Yeah? *Your* mama's so ugly, she has to tie pork chops to her legs to get the dog to play with her."

"Don't say. Well, your mama's so cross-eyed, when she drops a dime, she picks up two nickels."

"That's cold, but I'll tell you what. *Your* mama —"

You get the picture. And even before boys stride into such mean and endless jousts in school yards, parking lots, and other training grounds, every one of them gets the picture as well. Real men protect their mothers. For every kid old enough to make a fist, it's an instinctive and powerful reaction. For sons who have grown older, it's a gratifying method of looking out for their mothers and achieving their male status at once. The toughest, shiest, and most nonchalant among us rages against any danger to his mother. Just as a mother's impulse is to protect her baby, that baby grows to feel like her protector in return.

I'd never seen her look as impressive, as firmly and happily in total control, as I did one evening a few years ago. My mother stood straight-shouldered at the podium, a poster of her book jacket behind her, fielding questions on the history of apartment buildings. Nearly a hundred people had hustled into the small auditorium to hear her speak, and they were laughing at her quips, nodding deeply at her theories. But no one was as profoundly stirred as I was, seated near the middle and craning my neck. Then a white-haired man a few seats from me raised his voice to question her chronology. My mother responded to him mildly, smiling her allowance of different interpretations, and motioned to the next raised hand. But the man pressed on. He grew louder, barking out a challenge.

I don't remember his point—something about the height laws of the last century or the architectural record of Central Park South—but I still can recall the wrath that tightened his face, the gentleness that left hers open, and the boiling heat that puffed into mine as I watched this poisonous bookworm assault my mother in her finest hour. I could almost punch him without standing up if I leaned all the way forward and swung wide. Or else I could tackle him in three quick steps, take him down amid the metallic applause of folding chairs. But that was silly. What was this piping fury that nearly drove me from my seat? Why would I bodily attack a member of the audience for posing a rather vigorous question? Because any harm to my mother was a call to arms. Like most men, I may have had trouble vocalizing my devotion to my mom; but when challenged, I was thrilled at the chance to prove it. Of course, in the oak-paneled sitting rooms of civilized life, such a base, physical display would not be permitted. I had no outlet for the fury thumping through me—except a very small one. Weaving through the crowded room after the talk, I poked the gentleman covertly in the ribs with a single index finger—and then moved along, beaming as I approached my mother.

When they can stick up for their moms more publicly than that, sons leap at the opportunity and celebrate it long after. "I remember the best day I ever had," boasts Patrick. After a divorce when Patrick was one, his mother remarried into a rocky union that brought mother and son even closer than they'd been. It was this marriage that was ending, in ugly fashion, the day Patrick came home from his junior year at boarding school. "I'd been playing football, lifting weights every day, and I'd turned myself into 192 pounds of muscle," he reports proudly. So when a loud dispute between his mother and stepfather over the car keys turned physical, for the first time in his life, Patrick placed himself boldly before her.

"I just stood there and said to him, *Let it go. Just let it go,*" he remembers. "He looked at me. And I looked at him. And then he let it go. And that felt pretty great." It's the sort of showdown that's featured in the daydreams of countless sons; but more often than not, only there.

Usually, a son's ongoing battles on his mother's behalf are less dramatic than Patrick's. In fact, most of the time they're invisible. Lloyd's safeguarding of his mother was so secret, for instance, that it still mystifies him. Before and after Lloyd left home, there was so little affection between himself and his mother that he repeatedly waved off my request for an interview. "You don't want to hear from me," he insisted. "I'm not going to be much help to you on mothers and sons." But in the course of our conversation, Lloyd is forced to reconsider his relationship with his mother, startled by a recurring, subconscious event from his childhood.

"It's a dream I had over and over, and it's the one I remember most vividly, even now," he says. In the dream, his mother is being laughed at harshly by an anonymous crowd of people, and Lloyd is attempting to shelter her. And while he can recall neither the reason for the ridicule nor whether he succeeds in protecting her, he still is moved by the piercing sense of her vulnerability and his own need to remedy it. "I suppose that the dream suggests that there was love there, and an affection that wasn't part of my conscious awareness," Lloyd allows, "if you believe in that sort of thing." Meanwhile, he makes quite clear that he does.

Guarding a mother against all life's risks is as hopeless an endeavor as a mother's permanent harboring of a son. Despite a son's best and best-concealed intentions, there is little chance of hoisting her completely out of harm's way—particularly when he is older and no longer often by her side. As a result, the protective zeal of sons turns bitter. This is often the only evidence of our vigilant watch: our anger and silence when it is foiled. Just as a mother must quiet her urges to keep her son sheltered, her young man will hide his struggles in her defense. He does not let her in on his bodyguarding duties, as she is to be kept absolutely safe and clear from the brawl. But men's protective bouts are very real and very painful, since their mothers' foes are their own foes and they seem to be everywhere.

.　　.　　.

Some people smoke like they know that they're in error. They take a quick pull and thrust it away, a dirty cloud thrown upward before speaking, the cigarette back into hiding by a hip. My mother, on the other hand, used to smoke as if she were cradling pleasure itself. Her eyes would half-close around the thing, and as she exhaled she held it aloft as if presenting a specialty dish. For her, she once told me, smoking recalled the days of three-martini lunches with crotchety journalists, the all-night bistros in Paris, grand afternoons in vintage New York. For her sons, however, it meant guerrilla warfare.

In a free country, as she often pointed out, she had every right to one minor and legal vice—except that it infringed on our masculine right to look out for her. So the three of us implemented a multipronged defense both for my mother and against her. We started by buying her gum: a pack or two at first, then the economy-size holster of the stuff, and before long her bedside drawer was too full to close. Soon Luke began to discard every stray cigarette and pack that he came across, becoming an expert at hunting them out. When my mom bought more, hiding them and herself in her study to puff away, Jake invented thirty reasons a day to walk through and interrupt her, then sniff the air and cry foul. She began to take more frequent walks outside. As a last resort, I dripped her fancy facial cleanser into countless tobacco tips, then closed and replaced the packs in their usual spots. And at long last, it all took effect. Terrorized from all sides, my mother gave in, threw out the last soggy stashes, and turned to her closetful of gum.

What is striking is that, with all of our schemes, none of us thought to tell my mother simply how we felt: deeply disturbed by her assault on her health, agitated by the peril that she was happily buying by the packful. Any damage to a mother is a failure of her sons. Therefore, we become furious at our mothers' harmful habits, chronic injuries, and vulnerabilities of all kinds; but we keep quiet in our fury. Shame and anger combine to halt our speech even as it prompts our actions. Men are not expected to discuss how severely they are hurt each time their mothers are hurt: they are expected to prevent it. Once, our moms stood up loudly to mean teachers and neighborhood bullies for our sakes. Now it's our turn to defend them, with fewer words but equal passion.

While Charles was at college, two things happened to jeopardize his protection of his mother. First, having divorced when Charles was young, she married a man who began to treat her badly. Then, while her son was still a newcomer on campus, she was in a car accident that left her bedridden for months. "I wasn't there for my mom during all that," Charles laments. "It was a bad experience for me, knowing that something was wrong and not being able to do anything about it. I didn't know how to deal with not being in a position to stick up for her." Feeling that he'd abandoned his post by his mother, Charles felt guilty. But feeling that college should be a time of outward movement, he swallowed that homeward pang—and all other communication with it.

"There was this huge block in our conversations," Charles realizes now. "I was caught up in college life and was in a band and doing my own thing. But at the same time, I was hurting because I could tell my mom was hurting. She didn't tell me all the details, but I could tell. That was definitely the low point in our communication." Her new husband was stranding her all day long and not looking out for her emotionally; meanwhile, she was disregarding her own feelings as well by keeping her distress to herself, out of respect for the purity of Charles's college experience. With her keeping mum and her son keeping cool, the silent standoff between mother and son continued until she separated from her husband.

"It wasn't until I went to help her move out," Charles says, "that I realized what bad shape she was in—and how bad I'd been feeling about not being able to save her from her problems. There's no way to talk about it and no way to accomplish it, I know. But it's not a rational thing. I just wanted, very badly, to keep her safe from hurting."

Owing Our Lives

As a mother, there's no sense of being put out, really. I had no regrets about giving it everything I had, putting other things aside for the sake of my son. He was this tiny boy, this unbelievable gift, and I felt grateful to have him. I would literally give my life for him. There's no way to understand that feeling until you become a mother.

The sensation is astounding, but it is not exclusive to mothers. Sons of all ages and upbringings share a vast, natural gratitude to their moms that leaves themselves at a loss. Without our mothers, of course, none of us would have happened. It's thanks to them that we were cared for in the past and equipped for our futures; but our thankfulness does not come into focus until we become independent. And by then, we've lost our boyish ability to express it.

Immersed in manhood, we attend course after course on how to act responsibly. Men, according to the lectures of other men, have to earn a living, pay back loans, credit sources. Our relationships, both personal and professional, are matters of give and take in equal measure. Everyone owes someone and works to be legitimately owed himself. As we stride forth into the swarm of these adult equations, we cannot help but be struck by our obligation to our mothers. But how can we put a price on what she's given us, let alone repay her?

As children, we once took stabs at it. With childlike enthusiasm and adult supervision, we made odd and valiant attempts to gift-wrap our gratitude, heaping crayon masterpieces and tributes in raw macaroni at our mothers' feet. But it doesn't take long for sons to grow out of that stage and into greater difficulty. Rocking on the waves of early adolescence, for instance, I poured out a long poem to my mother for her fortieth birthday. It came from the depths of my growing soul and was, without a doubt, horrendous. I can recall, with sickening clarity, only two lines, wherein the poet describes his maternal muse as "transplanted oft to foreign lands / By crescent thoughts and hardy hands." Bestowing such gaudiness, penned in loopy script on typing paper—a medium that seemed, in my pretyping days, rather fancy—I felt awkward. When she read it and gave me a crooked smile, I felt off-base. And watching her tuck the thing away to the muffled snickers of the rest of my family, I felt certain that I should have stuck with uncooked pasta.

It's a gracelessness that's relived every Mother's Day. May brings a canned cornucopia of handy gifts and a broadcast sense that it's the least that sons can do. In truth, it's even less than that. The quickie gifts that clutter every store and catalog suggest that twenty-four hours on the calendar or twenty-four dollars on a credit card can clean the slate until next spring. And while it's perfectly pleasant to be granted an official day to be nice, we would prefer something more appropriate. The problem is not that the presents are too slick or too small, but that hand-held bunches and boxes have so little to do with what they've given us. It's not that Mother's Day should be every day, in which case it would lose whatever shrink-wrapped luster it has. It's that we are flailing for a more satisfying way to give back.

Keith, who works as a corporate consultant, sits behind a big desk in his large office as we speak. Not yet thirty, he already can claim his own personal assistant, a long and impressive list of clients, and a few minutes to talk before meetings and conference calls swamp the rest of his day. "My mom takes up a ton of my energy," he says. With rolled eyes and sagging shoulders, Keith describes long phone sessions, mandatory visits home, and his thoroughgoing efforts, as eldest son, to solve her financial and emotional dilemmas. But as he explains, his occasional irritation and exhaustion make his efforts more fitting. "It's pretty tiring, but I do feel like it's fair. I mean, should it be any different than what she had to offer me, even when she happened to be tired or annoyed?" Keith asks. "Of course not. How could I not be there for the one person who literally brought me into the world? I don't have any other relationships, including my relationship with my wife, that are like that. There are certainly no business relationships on that level." Every day, Keith takes account of the debits and liabilities involved in major transactions; yet the deal with his mother confounds him. "You can't measure the obligation to a mother," he concludes. "You can't. Just making an effort to be a good son; that's what I give back. That's why I try to be there for her, on the phone and in person. What else can you do?"

Many of us ask the very same question. We are spurred by a sharp sense of debt to our mothers but clueless at how to even the score. Few of us come up with any better offering than our company, a repayment that may seem meager—but is, in fact, quite suitable. More than anyone else in our lives, our mothers simply were there for us. Supportive or critical, constant or near-constant, our mothers' reliable presences were their gifts to us as we grew. And it's in eager attempts at justice that we give them our presences in return.

If all this seems suspiciously sunny, men think so too. Therefore, they make a point to gripe and groan about it. When I used to come home for the weekend, my routine was refined and firmly set: I dressed as sloppily as I could, parked myself in the same corner of the same couch, and read a teetering stack of magazines in front of the television until my eyes fogged over or dinner was served. Meanwhile, my mother would garden. It's an odd verb whose meaning I was slow to grasp, as I hardly ever assisted despite her often needing a hand. She'd have to call inside two or three times before I raised my head, issue three or four official requests before my body unfolded to standing position, then make a final plea to force me to walk myself outside. From her point of view, what was my problem? What could be more relaxing than to breathe among the scented rows of mint and chives? What could be more macho than to manhandle an oak or help her hammer in a fence post? From my point of view, the thought of helping her with yard work was more than un-

appealing: it was downright offensive, a threat to my independence and my adulthood. I happened, at the time,
to be interested in doing very little. And as an independent man spending an adult weekend, I had every right
to follow my interests.

Recently, however, my instinct has changed. I suppose
I've become less interested in singing out my rights and
more interested in doing right by her. I used to feel bogged
down and stifled by all I must owe her, and could relax
only when I kept my eyes from the imbalance. Now, on
the other hand, I feel more comfortable addressing my
mother's occasional needs than ignoring them. It's a no-
tion of fairness, more than her echoing call from the backyard, that makes me drop my reading and hustle out to
weed. It's out of a specific sense of righteousness, not out
of the general goodness of my heart, that I offer to prune
or water before she issues her ninth request. I am obligated to my mother, a fact and a feeling that no longer op-
presses me. That I cannot make up the difference is far
less important than giving it a shot, one trip to the garden
at a time.

The gaps and imbalances between Todd's parents are
not horrific, he is quick to point out; probably nothing out
of the ordinary. Married couples have fights. Inequalities
persist between men and women. But to a son eager to

show allegiance to his mom, they all are calls to quiet action. "If the lawn mower is broken the weekend I come home, and I fix it and mow the lawn," Todd explains, "it's to make up for the fact that Dad would never mow. When I cook dinner every so often, I'm making up for the fact that Dad doesn't cook and she always has to. And when I sit on the porch with her and we smoke while I ask her questions, it's to give her someone to vent to. I want her to be able to lean on me a bit." As an only child, Todd felt guilty when he left home, and now he takes comfort in attending to his mother each time he returns. But he is not obvious in his attentions.

"I'd bet she thinks that when I help out, I'm just entertaining myself or swept up in a big family weekend," he says. "But the truth is that I want to provide her with some help and some companionship. She did that for me, every day, for eighteen years or so. So I'm still heavy in the debt column. I want to even things up a bit, for my own peace of mind."

When Arthur was in his thirties, he was offered a more exciting job in another city. However, he turned it down, unbeknownst to the mother who was his reason for doing so. "The job was at a magazine that I liked and believed in," Arthur says. "And I would have been happy, I knew, in D.C. It represented a chance to get back into the political world, which I would have been excited to do." On the other hand, Arthur would have had to move away to Washington just as his mother was coming to settle near him. The decision weighed heavily on him for weeks: a heartfelt obligation, based on his past, versus an intriguing opportunity that led to the future. Ultimately, and thunderously, it fell on the side of his mother.

"I felt it in my gut. It would be better for her if I stayed; so I was staying. I was afraid that she would be isolated, and I wanted to be here for her."

When Arthur declined the job, his would-be employers were shocked. He was surprised as well—not at his choice, but at how satisfying it felt: "I knew it was the right thing to do. There were no real regrets, even though I might have expected that there would be. And I never told my mother about it. I wasn't looking to gain points. But I did feel like I owed her that."

Every so often, a man comes up with a more concrete scheme to repay his mother. For instance, even before she gave her son company, every mother gave him life itself—and that's a donation that, as astonishing as it is, there's a way to match.

"My mother wants grandchildren," says Victor. As he approaches thirty-two years old and his fourth anniversary with his wife, talk in the family has landed more and more often on the subject of a next generation. "My mother won't quite say it," Victor says, "but she makes little references to children all the time. And I'll give her grandkids. That's one of the things you owe, as a son. I have no problem with that." Having married his high school sweetheart, Victor is looking forward to a large family and to what it will mean to his mother. "My family will be a continuation of her, in a way. She brought me into life, and now I'll have children to bring to her. It's like a wonderful report card to show her. She'll see in the kids that all her work with me paid off. She'll see herself and her love in them, and that's enormously important to me. It's hard to explain how great that will make me feel."

The mute and grateful sons of mothers come up with a variety of repayment schemes—none of which is precisely that. A son gives her his company because she did the same; however, men do not go through life turning down all opportunities elsewhere in order to stick near their mothers. We speak of giving her grandchildren, but this is a momentous event that belongs to us. In any case, no mother stands impatiently in the way of her son, her arms outstretched for some payback. They retreat, as necessary, to watch men's performances and be fulfilled by them. Therein, at last, lies a reward big enough to be shared.

Both we and our mothers have mixed emotions as we gain independence; feelings of responsibility, confusion, eagerness, protectiveness, and obligation that grip us in private. But both of us have to release ourselves from such brooding. Our mothers know, and we learn from them, that as men we are supposed to think of ourselves and move along. We must please our moms through our achievements and not instead of them, by expanding our horizons rather than expressing all that pops up in our heads. It's a simple yet difficult resolution to the hidden anxieties of young men: A good son is one who lives his life well.

And in our effort to do so, we look for love.

CHAPTER FOUR

THE SILENCE: GIRLS, WOMEN, AND SEX

I CONFESS: WHEN MY MOM CALLED WITH AN EDITO-rial suggestion, I didn't take it too seriously. "Isn't there a lot to say about girls?" she asked. "I mean, *I* always wondered. Are you making sure to include plenty on sons' love lives?" Stiffly, I informed her that it was in the book, not to worry. When I spoke to a few more mothers about the project, however, I was barraged with the same advice. The call was multiplied by phone, letter, and fax, as the moms who counseled me acted increasingly like—well, like moms, pressing me for more about our love lives than the author or subjects had thought to include. And I, in response, acted like a typical son, shutting up and shutting out the clamor for this chapter.

How come the first instinct of young men—author

included—is to give their moms the silent treatment when it comes to affairs of the heart? Why all the secretive muttering and half-answers, the full about-face to subjects apart from women? Mothers are the only people we know who have years of firsthand experience both in our personalities and in the opposite sex. Wouldn't they be likely advisors? Nor are boys, in general, against discussing such matters. Sex and relationships are staples of our conversations from bunk beds to bar stools, and even, in private moments, with our fathers. Why, then, does nearly every son wall off his mother, the chief engineer of his primary male-female relationship, when it comes time to build others of them?

Our secrecy as we date and don't date is prompted by three factors, all of them familiar, none of them discussed. We are haunted by a dark taboo that surrounds our mothers and keeps them from all things sexual; we are swept up in the lore of our own independence, determined above all to cement our autonomy; and we are bothered by a false fable that our mothers seem willing to heed: the incorrect assumption that they are soon to be replaced. Through these three vehicles, culture and myth combine to keep young men tight-lipped when it comes to speaking with our mothers about love.

The Big Taboo

My mother was in bed. She'd gone upstairs about a half-hour before I left my father, asleep before the television, to turn in myself. It was my first vacation from college, and I must have been feeling sentimental because I decided to pass through my parents' room on the way to mine. Her reading light was off already. I leaned down and kissed her cheek good night, and as I moved away she mumbled something, her eyes still closed. "Huh?" I bent back down toward her. That's when she drawled, "Not tonight, honey, I'm so tired."

I must have jumped back half the length of the room, landing in the quiet darkness. My stomach whirled, my hands at my chest. The primal taboo had roared up from that bed and punched me full force. For a groggy second my strict and separate categories had merged, sex and my mom grotesquely fused in the same utterance. She'd mistaken me for my father; but it was I who was somehow horribly wrong. I scurried to my room, light-headed and sluggish with guilt. Despite being rattled, the division between my mother and such intimacy was not broken down that night. It was intensified, from that dreadful instant on, with all the force I could muster.

The very thought is so raw, so utterly blasphemous, that few have dared even to make up stories about it in the centuries since Sophocles. It's so thunderously forbidden that it paralyzes the loose talk and kidding of seasoned adults. And it's so resounding a taboo that it stiffens the conduct of men our whole lives. Sex and our mothers are to be kept entirely separate. We learned it early and forcefully, and the lesson is one that doesn't fade. Undeniably, almost every young man has a rampant interest in sex. Irrefutably, every last one of our mothers must have had sex to have us. Yet in the event that those two realms even graze each other momentarily, it all short-circuits—and silence ensues.

As interview after interview drew to a close, I could count on hearing certain questions in return. Mothers would ask me specifically about their own sons; sons would inevitably ask me what other guys said; and practically everyone would ask me about Oedipus: "Is it, you know, real?"—in a whisper, with a laugh. "Have you found that there's something to it? Or not?" The query comes tentatively from women, apprehensively from men—and therein lies the answer. Oedipus is real, like the bogeyman, as long as we fitfully believe him so. And we do. Sons are uneasy about sex and our mothers not because we are fatefully attracted to them, but because we are determined not to behave in the least bit so. Rest assured, every son is not the main character of that legend. But as for the taboo that is its moral, every one of us knows it by heart and acts accordingly.

The Oedipus complex is a much-mentioned affliction that's cured over and over before it can even occur, thanks to shock therapy. For example, when Alex accidentally failed to separate his mother and sex, he was jolted. The clash occurred when his mother, putting away clothes, found a condom in her seventeen-year-old's clothes drawer. "That was really rough," he says. "My response was just like, *Oh, man*. I didn't know what to think, other than, *My* mother *knows that I'm having sex with somebody. My* mother."

Neither Alex's upbringing nor his mother's attitude had been particularly puritanical. She had instructed her daughter about sex and was pleased that her younger son was actively dating. However, this event marked a blatant violation. "Your mom's not supposed to be in on that stuff," Alex affirms. "It bothered her, too. She didn't like the thought that I'd had sex—and was apparently planning to have more sex—in her home. But it totally embarrassed me." It so upset him, in fact, that it ruined his newly sexual relationship with his girlfriend for weeks.

"I was really thrown. I couldn't have sex then, even though I wanted to," Alex admits. "I just couldn't stop worrying about it. Your mother's not supposed to be involved in sex, on any level. That's all I could think."

To mix or muddle our moms and romance, even by oversight or in a casual chat, represents a threat to our crucial world order. This is why we go to the opposite extreme. It's far easier to avoid hugging our mothers altogether than to come up with some perfectly acceptable embraces whose physics and duration keep clear of anything too intimate. It's better to whack our bedroom doors shut than to debate the acceptability of our mothers spotting us half-dressed. And it's much safer to remain absolutely mute on romance than to dance around the risk of sharing just a little bit too much.

So what's the huge and looming risk? What's the fear that halts all affectionate mother-son displays and bars all adventurous heart-to-heart talks? Despite how it might appear, it is not our moms' interest in us that sends us scurrying off, but rather the remote danger of the inverse. Boys in adolescence, just learning the fearsome power of male hormones, are more wary of themselves than of their mothers. After all, we're the ones with the unwieldy new libidos and half-formed sexual identities; what if they go awry? Young men are even less comfortable with the thought of listening to their mothers' romantic news than they are when pressed to reveal their own: wouldn't boys' close attention reflect an inappropriate curiosity? If it's a crime for a son to allow his mom into his most intimate endeavors, then it's a graver offense to trespass into hers, regardless of any reason or invitation. Boys subconsciously vow to keep themselves in their places, and thus displace open communication between sons and mothers.

"I don't ask her about who she used to date and whether she used to score," says Randall. "That's repulsive. So she shouldn't ask me about it." As he's grown to thirteen years old, Randall has learned not to cross certain lines, and to be outraged when his mother does. "I'm not going to tell her about girls and all that," says Randall. "She'll ask me all the time, *Who's the special lady these days? Do you like Danielle? Do you like Wendy? Who's this Shauna?* She tries to get into it with me, but I keep her out." His parents divorced early on, and Randall has enjoyed an honest and dynamic relationship with his mother ever since. Yet as he has turned adolescent, his mother's attention has turned to his female classmates, and he has turned defiant and silent. "That's not her business, definitely," he says. "Girls? That's not a mother's place. That's man-to-man stuff, definitely not man-to-mom. *Definitely.*"

For Eric, too, it's a glaring omission in a relationship that's otherwise wide open. "The only thing I don't talk to my mom about is sex," he says, "because she'd want to talk *back*. And I don't think so. I don't open those doors." At twenty-two years old, Eric has always prided himself on being up front with the woman who raised him. "Everything else, me and my mom will talk back and forth about," he boasts. "I mean *everything*, just like friends. But I don't want to go there with my mom, in terms of sex." Regardless of what his mother might think, Eric is not that interested in protecting any secrets of his own. More fervently, he's against his mom's revealing herself to him. "I'd even be more at ease telling her about *me* and sex than hearing about *her*," he says. "But I'd rather not chance that by talking about anything close."

Gary also delineates the way a son's supposed to. "A mother is supposed to be a mother, and a son a son," he declares. "A mother is supposed to be a figure of authority at first, a nurturing figure, a provider. But my mother, particularly as I have grown into my twenties, is always seeking to make me a confidant. She doesn't hold enough back. She thinks that anything goes with me." For instance, she jokingly revealed to him that he was conceived underneath the dining room table, and refers occasionally to the sexual appetite of Gary's estranged father. In response to such disclosures, her son finds himself cringing. "One of the most chilling things she ever said to me was, *It's so good to know that after all we've been through, I have a son that I can share anything with,*" Gary says. "That kind of intimacy, at my age, feels incestuous." There are boundaries that simply may not be crossed or questioned, sharp fences that keep all talk of sex and bodies away from the woman whose sex and body gave us life.

However, sex is not the whole story when it comes to romance. Eventually, with any luck, young men's love lives progress beyond their sex lives. Therefore, at that point, why doesn't the boundary dissolve? With serious relationships come issues of commitment and compromise, deeper questions of emotion and character with which our mothers could more comfortably help us. Why, then, don't we let them? Because sons have spent year after formative year practicing tactics of exclusion rather than practicing conversations with their moms about relationships. By the time the boyish obsession with sex recedes to allow for a kosher, fruitful mother-son talk on love, most boys don't know how to start. Boys have obeyed and enforced the first taboo they learned with the help of a handy lack of language; now, unhappily, that's all they have. This is not the righteous silence of teenagers, but the frustrating speechlessness that it leaves, years later, in its wake.

Coupling on Our Own

In order to grow up, sons must grow autonomous; and this is the second reason why they grow silent as well. Men become distinguished, of course, by dividing between the family lives they inherit and the new lives they build from the ground up, according to their own plans. These are the unequal halves, dependent and independent, of a man's life. At the heart of each is a loving relationship with a woman—but these are two vastly different relationships with two wholly separate women. A man cannot allow his first love, as enormous as it is, to spill into his next; not only because such a merging is taboo, but because it would blur his personal and individual success. While a boy's relationship with his mother blends her

THE SECRET LOVE OF SONS

feelings and ideas with his, a man's courtship has to be pursued without maternal influence. To make sure that it is, we keep it completely to ourselves.

It was a long and top-secret time before I allowed my mother to meet my girlfriend. At first she'd ask me casual questions, steel-trapping the new name and occupation that were the only tidbits I'd offered. Was I bringing *her* for the long weekend? Would *she* be at the birthday dinner, the book party, the play? I realized, vaguely, that I was keeping this woman out of my mother's line of sight. The intention was to keep her fully and carefully in mine. After all, I figured, it was about time. When I was a baby, my mom arranged for playmates and knew my tastes as well as I did. When I was younger, I presented my ice skating partners and PG-movie dates to her with pride, pleased to have come up with girls worthy of her attention. Now, on the other hand, I had to herald the dawn of romantic adulthood. I was different now, in my twenties and in love. This relationship was to be mine, and I had to secure it as such before sharing it—especially with the woman from whom I once could hold nothing back.

In order to fall in love, a son must make a bold departure from the days when he was cushioned by a very different sort of female affection. His mother's love bathed him unconditionally since birth. Now another woman's love must be fished for in a step-by-step process that's supremely conditional. His mother used to make him the precious center of attention; but to earn another woman's attentions, he has to learn not to be so self-centered. In this bracing contrast lies a challenge for sons, a key to adult fulfillment, and a likely communication gap between them and their mothers. But what are we thinking as we navigate that gap?

"I think that a mother's dating advice to her son would be so tainted by her own love for him that it could never be good advice," Julian theorizes. As a result, he takes pains to disregard her. "She's not in the loop at all with girlfriends," he states. "Zero. Not at all. When it comes to questions like, *Should I ask her out?* or *I saw her kissing Johnnie, what should I do?*—not even close. I've never looked to her for that. That's the cutoff I make." Julian's cutoff, like that of so many sons in their late twenties, throws his mom in with the warm old days of love taken for granted, blocking her from the new era of hot pursuits and cold calculations. "With my mother, the initial reaction is always going to be, *But you're the best in the world. How dare she . . .*" he says. It's a celebrated and documented fact that maternal encouragement helps a son along in life; what's less well-known is that it can backfire on him when it comes to love. "For almost thirty years my mom has drilled into me that I'm special above all other people," Julian reports, "and that attitude is not going to get me places with women. If for thirty years she'd been drilling into me, *Women are great no matter what they do,* then it'd be easier for me to find a girlfriend. As it is, I have to leave her out of the game. I have to play this one myself."

Jeremy also is eager to distinguish his new autonomy in matters of the heart. Therefore, just out of college, he bridles at his mom's questions. "She has this habit of always asking me, *Are you having fun? Is everything all right? What's going on with the girls?* She always wants to know more than I'm telling her," he says. "And my reaction, especially in the last couple years, isn't great. I guess I perceive her questions as lessening me. I feel like I'm grown up now and don't need them. She makes me feel like something must be wrong, with all those girl questions, when nothing's actually wrong." Jeremy's mother has always rooted for his success in all sorts of relationships; but never before has he revolted against her concern. "I guess I get pissed off," Jeremy admits, "and eventually I raise my voice and I'm like, *Don't ask me so many damned questions!* And then my mom gets upset and thinks that everything she's ever done is wrong. But I'm not totally down on her." His true anxiety, obscured by his outbursts, is directed at his own capability, not his mother's curiosity. "You want to feel like you've got the dating thing under control," Jeremy explains. "You don't want to have to account for everything and be double-checked all the time by your mom."

I, for instance, felt double-crossed when it happened. Don't get me wrong: I'll be the first to admit that it wasn't much of a pickup line. But the woman was tall, beautiful, and only a couple of rows ahead of me; the plane had touched down, we'd been welcomed to Cleveland over the loudspeakers, and I could have sworn that my family was out of earshot. In any case, I had only a minute or two to come up with something before we were to be herded past the *'Bye, thank you, 'Bye*s of the crew and into a long, stale weekend with my grandparents—and it was out of my mouth before I'd thought through its content. "So . . . going to Cleveland?" I drawled, my hand braced casually against an overhead storage bin. She turned, her expression a perfectly blank reflection of my idiocy; but before she could respond, I heard the snicker of a younger brother. "Sooo . . ." he crooned, turning to my mother, "ya traveling on an airplane?" My mom doubled over in glee.

"Going to Cleveland," from that moment on, became my mother's metaphor for all my romantic endeavors, and to hear her most offhanded joke about it stabbed me with self-consciousness. If she ever wondered how my love life was going, she must have thought of that line and winced; but I winced harder. I was not that stupid or flailing, I swore. There were reasons, I suddenly understood, why men make such laughable attempts in the din of crowded bars and in the messy ruckus of parties, where their ineptitude can be swept away by the crowd—and where the older women who'd tracked their social progress most keenly were absent. Never again would I try so hard, say something so dumb, attempt flirtation during air travel. Or at least I would never, ever do so near my mother.

Michael's need to feel self-sufficient also hampered his communication with his mother. For six full years, he shut her out while he pursued and repursued a topsy-turvy relationship during and after college. "It was like I was on one of those Habitrail wheels, and couldn't get off," he admits. "I was crazy, dealing with that woman. And all my mother could say to me was, *You're going to have a nervous breakdown. What's going on?* But I wouldn't let her in enough to help. I know she wanted to, but I was like,

I'm fine. I can handle it, thanks. I wouldn't answer any of her questions."

When it comes to women, Michael believes, a man cannot rely on the one he's known since birth. "I think you have to make your own mistakes there, I really do. Your mother can guide you from a distance and maybe give you some framework, but when push comes to shove, a man's flying solo." However, he flies with a strong desire for his mother to follow his lead.

"It was a little weird for my mom, at first, that Kristen is black," says Seth, who's white. "I guess I've been exposed to lifestyles and ways of thinking and environments that are open and supportive and free, while my mother really hasn't. She's somewhat open-minded, but she was limited by her environment." While Seth is decidedly understanding now, back when he and Kristen became engaged, he was far less tolerant of his mother's opinion. "That was the roughest time I've ever gone through with her," he says. "I was really disappointed, and I let her know that loud and clear. She was being totally foolish and wasn't seeing things the way I was seeing them. I was the one in love, I was the one who was going to get married, and I wanted her support." When sons furiously defend their choices of partners, they make not only statements of individualism, but pleas for accompaniment. And at last, after arguments and awkwardness, Seth's mom listened to both—and regretted her racism. "She realized that she was being idiotic and apologized profusely," Seth says. "Now she loves Kristen and thinks she's a beautiful woman. I think that, as a son, you want your mom to love who you love, even though you might not admit that."

It's a subtle but emphatic distinction. Young men are not looking for women who will meet their mothers' specifications; they are looking for their mothers to adopt and celebrate their own. In fact, the need for maternal consent would be a blow to our autonomy, and thus is not permissible. As men, we would like our mothers' visions of our mates to meet our own; but we must get there individually, not obediently. Meanwhile, mothers must learn to appreciate our partners by following our cues.

With two older sisters who have married Jewish men and two more who have married Gentiles, Ben is, as he puts it, "the tiebreaker" in his Jewish mother's scorebook. "Somehow it's up to me, now, to prove that she raised us right, based on who I marry and what her religion is," he complains. "Deciding on marriage is hard enough without my mother inserting herself on the religious front."

He's been in an interfaith relationship for two years now and is considering getting engaged, despite his mother's objections. He has told her about his devotion to Jennifer; yet his feelings seem to carry less weight than his mother's religious convictions, leaving the two of them at odds and leaving Ben offended. "Listen, I'd like to marry someone Jewish, too," he says, "but that's not more important to me than whether I love the person or not. And if my mother were seeing things at all from my point of view, she'd ease up. If there's one thing in your life that a guy should be able to be selfish about, it's who you marry and spend the rest of your life with, whether she's green, blue, or orange."

Or male. Our romantic desires are up to us, in keeping with our own hearts and characters and nobody else's, and mothers who disapprove of our sexual preferences challenge that invaluable right to desire. Moreover, a gay man cannot help but be confused and hurt by his mom's eagerness to blame herself. It's a popular, knee-jerk response that's an offense, among other things, against his self-sufficiency. Her suggestion, doubly objectionable, is not only that he has developed askew, but that he has done so because of her unmasculine influence, not his own emotions. The repentant mother of a gay man seems to think that she must have tipped the scales or poisoned the petri dish; but he does not think of himself as a lab experiment or faulty product so much as the thinking, feeling producer of his very own mature relationships. Every man's search for mutual devotion beyond his family is personal. Whether homosexual, heterosexual, bisexual, or asexual, falling in love is our sole responsibility and solo endeavor, for better or for worse.

"My mom would take the blame for Chernobyl, if she could," says Phillip. "But that made things a lot harder for me when I came out of the closet to her, in my twenties." What bothered Phillip was her implication that she must have done something wrong—at precisely the moment when he felt, at last, that he was doing things right. "This was just the hand of cards I was dealt in this life," he says. "I was born gay, and I was sorry if that made her insecure. But for the first time in my life, I felt secure about it." As Phillip moved to a new neighborhood, developed new friendships, and relaxed into his new and fulfilling lifestyle, his mother was unwilling to respect his self-determination. Therefore, Phillip had to demand it. "At some point I had to tell her, *Please. If you want to entertain yourself with your guilt, fine. But I'm the one who's responsible for my life.* And she listened." Over a recent holiday weekend, Phillip hosted family and friends and was rewarded for his efforts with his mother's enthusiasm. "She said to me after Christmas, right as she was leaving, *You've done good for yourself,*" Phillip recalls. And that was a greater gift than he had ever received from her.

The Myth of Mothers Replaced

My mother wanted me in the picture. It was to be a family portrait, after all, taken by a photographer friend to celebrate my parents' recent move back to New York City. It was also to be snapped at the moment I planned to be halfway to Virginia to visit my girlfriend, in graduate school there for a year. I was caught. Not to see my girlfriend would mean postponing our reunion another exasperating week. Not to be in the photograph would mean enduring immortality as a gap in the cheery lineup of my family. Of course, I chose to head south—because mothers are famous for sticking around anyway, and girlfriends are famous for not. But in fleeting moments that weekend and after, I felt sick about it. When my mother asked nicely about my Virginia visit, I could muster no pleasant chit-chat. *He's on his way out,* I heard between her upbeat lines. *I have the proof of his vanishing on film.* I was at once defiant and ashamed: I was doing nothing wrong, and hurting her by doing it. I felt proud of my blossoming romance, but my mom seemed to feel betrayed. There were no words for that; nothing, in any case, like the full story told by the portrait that was passed around a few weeks later. Two grinning guys stood by a father swelling with pride, while a mother, her expression hard to read, held a high school headshot of her oldest son, as if he had criminally disappeared.

The silence of socially active young men—enforced by a taboo, reinforced by autonomy—can be traced to a third source as well, this one as hazy and potent as the others. The common, melancholy yarn is that our mates replace our mothers. It's an age-old myth, recycled in popular culture by the comic demonization of mothers-in-law, reinstated in men's experience by any tension between the two starring women in their lives. Which is not to say that we believe it: we do not. As a young man juggles the presence of a girlfriend and that of his mother, awkward moments are inevitable, but they are not part of any plot for a brusque female substitution. While a son may opt to spend on a lover the time and energy that once was alloted to his mom, such decisions have much more to do with new limitations on time and energy than any drop in mother-son devotion. Like the tale of Oedipus, and like all the hullaballoo about men striking out on their own, this replacement theory is merely a tall tale that's passed on and on until it resonates.

Lewis is caught in the heat of the battle between his mother and his girlfriend; but, as he points out, it's baseless. "My thing with Beth and my bond with my mother are totally different relationships," he says. "There's no competition there. I'm not choosing one over the other. And even if I were, I certainly wouldn't be about to cast off my mom." Still, the excitement of his first serious relationship, at twenty years old, is being marred by his worries about his mom. "I sensed a tension right away between Beth and my mother," he says. "There haven't been any arguments between the two of them or anything, and there were never bad words or scowling. But you can feel it, and it comes from my mother." It comes in the form of her requests to plan weekend visits from college, complaints that he hurries off the phone to go out with his girlfriend, and her suspicious-sounding questions about Beth's background and interests. "I can feel my mom's hesitation," Lewis says. "It's easy to pick up on that; I know her pretty well. She has these feelings of abandonment; and just sensing that, I have trouble opening up to my mom about what's going on with Beth. It feels like I'd be throwing it in her face by talking too much about it."

Given the palpable awkwardness, Lewis has no desire to increase it by boasting about his girlfriend to his mother; but he does that inadvertently by clamming up. Meanwhile, his sincere aim is to debunk the myth of mother-lover rivalry. "I'm eager to show my mom that it's all bull, that I care about both of them, and that I'm the same guy with the same feelings that I've always been," Lewis says. "I don't want my mother to buy into the aging, lonely matriarch thing. Nobody's going to do that to her, especially me. That's only going to happen if she makes it happen."

Dean also felt painfully stretched into silence by his mother and his five-year-old relationship. "When things with Tracy got serious," he says, "I was kind of worried about my mom thinking that she was being left behind or something. That made things a bit awkward between us." Dean's anxious interpretations came to a head one day when Tracy noticed, out loud, that his mother had no pictures of the two of them in her house. "I got defensive of my mom," Dean says. "That was my reaction. I told Tracy to forget about it." Then, however, he was pulled the other way.

"Tracy was right, of course. It was true: not one snap-shot, after all those years. Meanwhile, Tracy's mom has had pictures of the two of us all over her living room. So I was forced to be like, *Wow, maybe my mom* is *holding on to me tightly. Could she really want it to be just me and her all my life? Could she be falling into that position?* And so I sort of avoided my mother for a while, with all that." At last Dean's mom scattered around a few photos of the couple, and the problem was solved—until a recent Valentine's Day, when Dean received a greeting card from his mother that didn't mention Tracy. "I was like, *Oh, shit. Here we go again. How could she be pulling this?*" he remembers. "And just then I looked over and there was a card for Tracy too. And I was like, *Thank God. It was nothing the whole time.*"

Lovers do not and cannot take a mother's place in a man's life, and those who might try only prove that neatly. Nobody wants a girlfriend who treats you like your mom does. In a son's estimation of a woman, there is a fine line between her doting and mothering, between her offering advice and offering a maternal substitute, that is not to be crossed. And the instant our lovers overstep into our moms' territory, they are out of place. Breakup after breakup occurs when young men begin to feel mothered by women who have no claim to that title. The reverence, scorn, and love that are our moms' inalienable rights cannot be displaced or transferred.

Now that he's married, less has changed in Keith's mind than his mother might think. "I suppose I've sort of replaced her, as far as she can tell," he considers, "since most of the female sustenance and input comes from my wife, suddenly, rather than from her. And that must be painful for my mom. But the thing is, that's not what's happening at all." The shift that's taken place is an expansion, Keith explains, rather than some straight exchange. True, he has not been able to come home as often as when he was single. As a matter of course, for instance, some of their traditional family ski trips have had to go by the wayside, as he's spent every other holiday at his wife's family's house instead of his mother's. "I have to balance requirements now," he says. "That's what marriage means: there are limitations and compromises. But as far as the emotional side of it, no way. Those are different realms. My mother and my wife each have a role, and I need both of them, not just one or the other."

A young man's goal is to maintain two different bonds with two different women, one who keeps a hold on his past and the other on his future. Therefore, to watch the happy coexistence of a mother and a mate is cause for huge—if hidden—celebration. Their bond serves as resounding proof that a son has adopted and applied the values taught by his first female influence. Their friendship is a tribute to his mother, to himself, and to the young woman who helps him accomplish the closure. He feels kindly and selfishly pleased, genuinely whole. And without it he feels incomplete.

My mother, by all rights, should love my girlfriend. They have plenty in common besides me: a passion for cities and a longing for country life; an itch to go to parties and a quiet need to sit home alone; a penchant for kooky outfits and fine arts and oddballs. They both have experiences with brothers, other countries, and all-female educations that would be worth sharing. By all accounts, they both are strong women—but my mother seemed not to see this woman's strengths, remaining politely aloof when I arranged for the three of us to have drinks for the first time. I tottered from one furious allegiance to the other, angry at my mother for not getting onboard, disappointed with my girlfriend for not pulling her in, sipping my drink as if all were going just swimmingly. I raised and threw around issues, names, and interests that would bind them like lassoes. I left them alone by going to the bathroom—three times. And when I got back from each trip I looked closely at my mom.

I did not need my mother's consent. I was, however, eager to dispel the myth that seemed to be bothering her, and impatient for the three of us to celebrate its defeat together. I was not about to vanish with this woman; I was planning to become more substantial, dependable, and expressive, with her help. I was in love; didn't my mom want to join me? I'd found someone to pick up where she'd left off, who was helping me grow up and grow better. Why wasn't my mother applauding the advance? I cannot pinpoint when the two of them began to talk in earnest or what prompted the warming of that room, the ultimate gaiety of that afternoon. But I do remember clearly the feeling as I watched them chat and laugh: a soft, full rest at the end of a tug-of-war that I'd fought by myself.

It's no wonder, then, that we may choose partners and wives who resemble our mothers, thus shortcutting our voyages to heartfelt closure. *Do men marry their moms?* comes the question from the women's side, half-worried and half-proud. *Absolutely not,* men gruffly retort. To do so would be triply intolerable: that would mean mixing moms and sex; smudging the line between boyish and manly loves; and replacing the one woman who cannot be ousted. Impossible, we shake our heads—until we consider the matter further. Well, often, it seems, it just happens to happen that way. Oddly, silently, and often to our own surprise, our mothers tend to reenter our love lives somewhere within the person we love.

"I definitely didn't look for my mother in a wife," Brian, now twenty-seven years old and engaged, says with a laugh. "I didn't go looking for someone who was the opposite of my mother, either. Meredith is neither, really." He thinks it over for a minute more. "Although—I guess you do get a certain appreciation for women, and for people in general, from your mom. The serious relationships I've formed have been influenced by her, probably without my knowing it." Brian's thesis slowly changes along with his expression. "When I try to picture Meredith in the role of a mother, my mom is the prototype, of course. So in that way she's had a lot of indirect influence. I do size up Meredith—privately, to myself—and use my mom as the gold standard." Ultimately, Brian concludes, it's a natural phenomenon. "You find characteristics in your mother that you really appreciate; we all do. And when we reach the point where we can choose our relationships and aren't born into them, then we keep those characteristics in mind. So it's not shocking that Meredith is like my mother in certain ways that I have decided I value."

At forty, and at first glance, Ryan sees things clinically. "My wife is an artist; my mother is an artist. My wife doesn't cook; my mother doesn't cook. But those are co-incidences. They're far from the same person." In fact, the two don't even like each other. As she often tells her son, Ryan's mother has always found his wife moody and im-patient. In return, the younger woman complains to her husband about his mother all the time. "She makes the point: *Look, you talk about what a wonderful person your mother is, and how nurturing and warm and friendly she was, and I don't see it. Don't expect me to give her the ben-efit of the doubt the way you can, because you've known her and loved her all along,*" Ryan recounts. "And she's right: she doesn't see it. Because the two of them are strikingly different."

However, after further discussion, Ryan reveals that he's been struck by something else. "A couple of years ago," he considers, "I noted that when I hugged my mother, her height and her breadth and the feel of her in my grip was the *same* height and breadth and feel-in-the-grip of the woman I almost married when I was eighteen, of the woman I lived with for ten years, and of my wife now." It's a connection that's striking, perhaps unsettling, and completely understandable, even to a son who's frightened away from such parallels. "The very first person that I was profoundly, seriously, totally committed to fit that mold," Ryan says. "So am I looking for my mother in a wife? Certainly not. Well, certainly not *consciously*. Maybe not even unconsciously—but maybe in an unconscious, unstated physical way." It is hard to affix with a label, as it is not commonly discussed; but it is an uneasy, irrational phenomenon that occurs again and again.

The question is not whether men actively search for their mothers among marriage prospects. They don't. What is noteworthy is that they so often find them there. The fabled laws of men, mothers, and mating are not to be broken or disregarded: our moms are kept separate, our achievements are kept distinct, and our mother-son bonds are kept sacred and unique. Yet often in the subtext, sneaking between and over the lines, are female similarities that we choose not to discuss.

Neil set out expressly to avoid such parallels, prodded in the extreme opposite direction by the grim model of his parents. "I wanted to have a very different kind of relationship with my wife than my father had with my mother," he reflects. "I didn't like his domineering personality, and I thought that one way to avoid turning out that way myself was to have a very different sort of marriage with a stronger type of woman." Neil may have gone overboard, however: his first marriage ended with a physical assault by his wife.

"It was an absolute failure of a jump-start," he admits. "It was a hasty decision, and a wrong one, to say the least. But the lesson's learned. Now I have a softer, more healthy relationship with someone who, I have to say, is very much like my mother."

As his new marriage has developed and flourished, Neil's perspective has expanded as well. "It's full circle—well, not completely full circle, because I'm a very different man from my father, and my wife is not the same person as my mother. But you can't get away from where you come from. That's the lesson. And where you come from, of course, is your mother."

Even more striking than withholding our romances from our mothers is the passion with which we do so. Our fervency is born from our struggle. It requires effort not to share our optimism and anxieties with the most familiar ear that's offered, and that effort is what makes sons' evasions noble and petty, emphatic and dead silent. We feel entitled to act rigidly, because that's how we feel without the comfort of an expansive mother-son connection. But we cannot dodge forever. The musty parables that we must beware for years ultimately are put away. In order to live honestly and wholeheartedly, we give up the eggshell walk around our moms and set out for broader progress, rewarding conversations, and stories involving our mothers that the two of us write ourselves.

CHAPTER FIVE

MEETING OUR MOTHERS

WORKING FULL-SPEED AND LIVING ON MY OWN, I had hardly any candid, thorough conversations with my mother; yet I was hardly opposed to them. In fact, there were many times I craved honest communication with her. But I was a grown-up. I had arrived: good job, place to live, life to keep up with. I was trying hard to earn my keep, to build an existence around myself—and trying not to look for the exits or even glance out the windows that would have brought me face-to-face with my mom.

Now that I think of it, of course, both the facts and my feelings were pushing me toward her. I was writing, first of all, and as an author herself, my mom could be of help. I worked in publishing as well, an industry she cares and knows something about. And I was planning a book about mothers and sons, her field of expertise three times over. But all these were a man's pursuits, none of his mother's business. Deep down, I felt I deserved the sort of whole-hearted support and emotional exchange that only my mom could provide; yet I would not allow her to provide it. Intellectually and sentimentally, I needed her input. But I had no time for real conversation with my mother, no room in my jam-packed independence for someone who held so big a place.

As it was, I was working to squeeze in a double exis-tence. My alarm clock was set for 4:50 A.M., shouting me out of bed to write for three dim hours before I reported to my editorial job. I was on my stumbling way to be-coming an author and editor. Midday dizzy spells in the office were a harmless side effect, the blue circles under my eyes a mere aesthetic nuisance. And like sleep and sanity, gratifying contact with my mother was put off. As self-deprivation brought me a vague sense of virtue, ex-cluding her served to martyr me further. I was on a rough road of my own construction and my own ambition, made rougher and more ambitious by cutting my mother out. What mattered was not my health or the state of my very oldest relationship, but how hard I labored at new pur-suits. And as I worked, so did my plan. Sluggishly my body and mind obeyed, my careers edged along. And my mother, proud and concerned, looked on from elsewhere.

This is real life, actual manhood at last. Sons grow, as hoped, to be full-fledged men with their own affairs. They cannot admit defeat or even faintness of heart, and certainly they cannot whine to their mothers about the pressures they feel. Adult sons have learned to keep their heads down and their noses to the grindstone. They are busy trying as hard as they can, and trying not to dwell on the inevitable question that must also occur to their mothers: How long can these male mind-sets endure? As they head off to the office, burrow into projects, bury themselves in whatever they choose to do, the self-segregation of men is encouraged and applauded by everyone, including their moms. But must it be permanent? After young men tear away from their mothers, what will heal the communication gaps that they create?

The answers are startling. We are caught off guard by odd urges to get in touch with our mothers. We are discombobulated by our sudden need to ask them personal questions and share our feelings. Our mothers, too, often are surprised by our spontaneous efforts and approaches. Neither of us is familiar with men who break back toward their moms. But it's just as inevitable, and far more fulfilling, than our earlier custom of breaking away.

This turnaround of sons is one of the revolutions that comes with maturity. It's not well-known, because it isn't performed with as much hoopla as the exodus that makes it necessary. The boys who rebel against maternal offerings are far more famous than the men who rebel by seeking them out; but their numbers and convictions are equally strong.

A man's reunion with his mother is sparked, quietly and universally, by four principal events in his life: the assembly of a family of his own; his growing desire for knowledge that's exclusively maternal; his ultimate fatigue with a life spent alternately tiptoeing and sprinting on track; and emotional mother-son reversals that come with a mother's aging. As these four changes unfold, so, in effect, do we.

Family Wisdom

The careful creation of a new family turns a man's sentiments to his mother, the human foundation of the family he's always known. Having children means having thoughts about other upbringings—whether half-remembered, like his own, or nearly unknown, like his mother's. But the return of a mother's son is just as emotional as it is informational. Husbands and fathers yearn for the comfort that they associate with their moms as they attempt to create it in their own families. They are learning new sorts of devotion, brands of love that may be more familiar to a mother than to her son. While we grew up, our mother's insights often occurred behind our scenes. It's not until we're grown that we call them to the fore.

My own burgeoning family is very much a work-in-progress, featuring—at last count—a future wife and a four-month-old puppy. Bulky decisions involving long-term settlement and two-legged children don't have to be made yet, but they loom. And to consider these foggy developments more clearly, I could use my mother's experience and ideas. She managed to be a full-time writer and full-time parent, a trick I will need to learn. She raised kids in the city and in the country; and although I was one of them, I could benefit from her comparative analysis. Even harder to know, as I research my lifelong options, are the emotions—the anxious joy of marriage, the marvel of kids—that she could come closer to describing for me than anyone. Frankly, as a young man, my path is strewn with plenty of male opinions, predictions, and feedback. It's my maternal source of wisdom that has gone untapped—and for long enough.

For Kendall, the wait is over. "I'm having conversations with my mom these days, at thirty-eight years old, that I *never* would have thought of having before," he says. "And that's only happened since I've been married." When Kendall and his wife, Jill, had twins a few years ago, Jill gave up her professional ambitions in order to raise them. Naturally, this has been the subject of many husband-wife discussions ever since; and although times have changed since Kendall's mom weighed such options, it's a parallel that her son draws and pursues.

"My mother was fully expected to stay home and raise the children," he says, "and there was no debate about it. But what I've learned from Jill, in *our* debates, is that that's not a trivial choice for a woman to make."

Rethinking the start of his original family as he starts a new one, Kendall has reapproached his mother with curiosities new to him. "I've asked my mom about what she may have traded in when she became a full-time mother, her professional plans and ideas about lifestyle, and how she felt about doing it," he says. "I'm learning a lot more about her than I thought I wanted to know." Before now, such conversations might have proven awkward for a growing son, as no one is eager to hear about regrets associated with his own birth. For a pondering father, however, the chance to learn more about parenthood and his mother at once is no longer to be missed.

As men's own families continue to expand, so do their visions of their mothers. Years ago, Bruce's mom disapproved of his lifestyle and religion, and he responded by moving hours away and communicating seldomly. But recently, and surprisingly, Bruce reached out. "I had this flurry, right after my first son was born, when I'd write Mom," he says. "I'd just tell her, *Thank you. Thanks for all you did for me.* We were both kind of shocked by it."

Growing up, Bruce thought his mother was self-involved and out-of-date. These days, however, he sees this attitude as shortsighted. "You cannot appreciate the sacrifices mothers make until you have children. My mom really did a lot, and that never hit me before. When you have kids, you can't help but reflect on what your mother went through, especially early on. And I've had a real reversal that way."

The reversal began, appropriately enough, when Bruce was upside-down. "It was really strange," he says. "I'd be playing with Scottie on the floor, you know, picking him up with my feet over my chest, and a flashback would suddenly come to me of my mom doing that with me. It didn't kick in until I was doing the exact same thing with my boy. I had him in the exact same position, and he was laughing the same way I used to laugh, and it just clicked: *Wait a minute,* Mom *used to do that for me!*" Now the father of three boys, Bruce is in warm and regular contact with his mother. Although they still argue over religion, they discuss many subjects previously untouched—including Bruce's sense of gratitude.

"It's a relief to express how thankful I am to her," he says. "I never did that before, because it was always tangled up with all my other reactions to her as my parent. Now, as a busy father myself, I see things differently. My mom worked hard to raise me, and she didn't go nuts. That's a damned good trick, and I couldn't appreciate it until I tried the same thing myself."

Sometimes it's the love for a daughter, specifically, that reignites a man's interest in his mother. "Having girls makes me think a lot more about my mom's childhood than I ever had before," says Arthur. He admits that when he had his first daughter, he was at a loss. In fact, it was his ignorance, both as a father and as a son, that inspired him to seek the broader education that his mother could provide. "Suddenly, when I had daughters," he says, "I didn't know what to do. I wanted to have some conception of what it's like to be a girl in a family. I'd only seen my brothers grow up, and although I could ask my wife, she was too busy and too tired, naturally, to talk much about it. My mom was the only woman I knew much about—but not enough." As a result, Arthur sought out her natural expertise.

"I had a lot more talks with my mom about her girlhood than I would have otherwise," he says. "She told me a lot about her past that I didn't fully appreciate, or even have any interest in, before then. I was relying on her, and she delivered."

Having boys, too, throws a switch in our feelings. By watching our own sons with their own mother, we call to mind the days we had shut out. "Every day, I see the connection between a mother and son," says Anthony. "It's an amazing thing to watch." One year ago, his wife, Martha, gave birth to a son; and observing the two of them, Anthony experienced a renaissance in his feelings for his mother. "Martha is raising this little boy of ours, and he's just crazy about her. He smiles all the time at her, and is all in her hair. He's just beside himself." Anthony's wife has taught their one-year-old the joy of the secret garden; and the infant has taught Anthony to reconsider his own beginnings. "There's a closeness there that's not like anything else," he says. "I realize that I've put that aside for a while, in my own case. But it's not something you lose."

Anthony's mother was bewildered, he laughs, by the visits and phone calls home that began about twelve months ago. "She figured I was just looking for diaper advice and childcare info," he says. "But those calls are to show her that I still remember how close we were, that I'm still looking to her for some back-and-forth between us. I'm no different than I was back then, in my heart. I'm no different than my boy with his mom. That mother-son bond isn't something that goes away."

To Know Ourselves

Sons and mothers. Mothers and sons. I gathered up everything I saw in my apartment. Notes—check. But are the two of us supposed to talk that methodically, so deeply, along the lines of my sober script? Tape recorder—check. But what place did the hiss of technology have between mother and son? I tucked a few transcribed interviews and scrawled paragraphs into my bag, went out the door eager and unsure. An adult man is not meant to hang on his mom's every word, certainly, nor to hang his career on her knowledge. But this book is based on my mom, and us, as much as it is on me. I needed her—although I wouldn't have said it out loud or on tape. She held the keys to my understanding of how I got where I was—out the door, at the moment, tucking away my own keys and checking my watch. In the interests of this project and this son, I had pre-arranged a vital, in-depth conversation with my mother. It would be an interview; but it was far more significant than that. I was taking the subway to a meeting that had been postponed, overlooked, and in the works for as long as I could remember.

In fact, the allure of such meetings occurs to sons long before they would ever take part in them. Young men tend to know their mothers well while knowing precious little about their lives, and the reasons are obvious and selfish. While a father's life story can be used as a blueprint, or at least man-to-man inspiration, a mother's path leads inevitably—and irrelevantly—to motherhood. In our years of frantic male apprenticeship, our moms are off-limits, as they are off all-masculine tracks to success. Sons are aware that they are neglecting to learn all about their mothers. However, long before they will be burned and provoked by that deficiency, they manage to shrug it off.

"I still find out things about her that I never knew, stuff I never asked, I guess," says Maxwell. And at twenty-four years old, that irks him—but not enough to prompt action. "There are things I want to ask my mom about, things I definitely *will* ask her about one of these days," he says. "A lot of times, facts about her come out when she's with me and one of my friends. There will be some question my friend asks her, and she'll answer, and I'll be thinking, *Wow, I didn't know that about my mom either.*" According to Max, some of his ignorance is his mother's fault. "She doesn't really advertise her life, like my dad might," he considers. "It seems like she doesn't tell me everything, because she doesn't think I should be too interested." But with further reflection, Max realizes that it's not she who halts their communication.

"I think I'm self-centered in a lot of ways," he confesses. "I'm so focused on: *What am I going to do with my life? How am I going to make it, and make ends meet?* You know, you sort of forget that your mother had a life before you came into the world—maybe because it's convenient to forget that. I just don't get the chance to go there, these days."

Eventually, and precisely when we want it, we get the chance. And those of us who are fortunate get as many chances as we want. As my first brief interview with my mother had gone rather well, I arranged a second one to take place over dinner. My mother seemed dressed-up, quick-witted, and was enjoying herself. Her face and stories were flushed by the occasion and by the candlelight of the French restaurant. We ordered drinks, and she went expertly to the point, recalling her family and discussing ours, pausing to remind me of my tape recorder. I cursed, fumbled and placed it on top of the table between our plates.

At first I cushioned my statements with a preamble: "Many sons I've spoken with seem to feel that . . ." She did the same, innoculating her responses with, "As a mother, one tends to feel . . ." But before long we tossed out these passports and roamed louder, looser, and closer to each other. She chatted about her high school dances, her grade-A college endeavors, and her post-graduate scholarships with a sense of humor and purpose that I wasn't familiar with. She turned her narrative to me, my father, my brothers, and herself with a fluency that was captivating. I flipped the tape and ran through every question in my notes and on my mind. But once the check came and the door opened and we darted off in different directions, I had one more. Why had this taken so long? As I walked slowly from the restaurant, my knowledge of parents and children, even women and men, seemed to have broadened ever so slightly. By the time I reached my block, my own life seemed to me reasonably—if not perfectly—arranged. Why hadn't she and I leveled with each other before now? What had captivated or repulsed us for all these years, keeping us amiably apart, to be clapped together, at last, by a book?

Even the most egocentric of sons awakens, sooner or much later, to the value of his mother's perspective. Growing boys are barraged with notions of individualism, solo accomplishment, and objective status; once they've plowed through those to adulthood, they can lift their heads and look around. After all, there's a lot in it for the self-interested man. By seeking out a mother's experience and ideas, a son gains a greater sense of his upbringing and thus of himself. By getting to know the woman that he assumed he's known since birth, he can learn much about family, memory, and the way people grow. No matter how, when, and why he's developed thus far, at the base of his zigzagging growth—if not always at its controls—is his mother. And eventually, to trace himself from his past to his future, he needs her once more.

Leon has a theory about it: "I think, as a man, I've had a natural need to feel that I know my own life better than anyone," he says. "At the same time, my mother's the one who keeps an even longer record of my life than I do. She owns the log. And that log has interfered with my self-definition." Every mother has the exclusive ability to recall her son's earliest experiences and represent them to him when she sees fit. It made Leon uneasy when he was young: "You don't want someone that close to you to have something on you," he explains. "As a boy, I didn't want her to see me hurt or watch me lose, and I wouldn't tell her any embarrassing stories. Because with your mother, you know you're going to hear about those moments for the rest of your life. They're entered in her log." As a result, he distanced himself from his mom for many years. He hardly spoke to her about their past, wincing at her old stories and careful not to provide new ones. However, now that he's middle-aged, Leon embraces these maternal powers.

"What you realize as you mature," he says, "is that there are many positive uses of that log. For example, insofar as you're—I hate to use the term *finding yourself*, but, well—coming up with what makes you happy, then you've got someone who can say, *I remember the trouble you had in second grade, when you cried in class. You never did like authority. So why are you putting yourself through this horrible job?* Only your mother can help you that way." And when they're old enough to admit they could use that help, men seek it.

After decades of focusing on themselves, many men broaden their scopes in the pursuit of greater understanding. Frank, for instance, always felt put out by the strictness of his single, Korean mother. "I felt like other kids got to hang out and be cool," he says. "But I was always the one who joined my friends late, after my mom made me clean the bathroom or something. The guys would be like, *Where were you?* Then someone would say, *Hey, does anyone else smell Mop & Glo?* and I'd be like, *No, man, not me.*"

Now Frank has become less mortified and more inquisitive about his mother's past and her adjustment to life in the United States. "Coming from Korea as a single woman must have been hard," he considers. "In the Korean language, for instance, there are different dialects according to whom you're addressing. Everybody knows their 'station' and behaves appropriately. But suddenly when my mom got here, she had all these American kids coming up to her and saying, *Yo, lady, you got the time, or what?* So she had to develop a thick skin." The thickening of skin led to a toughening of rules in her household, a process that Frank has made sense of only in his adulthood. "She felt very much like she was an agent in the corruption of her Korean son," he realizes, "unless she took a stand against it. Sometimes that may have manifested itself in arguments between us. It seemed to me like she was talking to herself out loud, just stating her position on something, and as a kid I couldn't relate to that. But now I can." Piecing together our mothers' pasts helps us piece together our own, and the desire to do so deepens as our history does.

It was in the back of an Irish pub that I was awakened. It was our third interview, and I was almost at ease as I slid into the bar-side table with my trusty tape recorder and my mother. I asked about her childhood and pressed play.

"In a lot of ways," she said, "I come from the school of straight and narrow, as you know." I did know bits and pieces of her upbringing: the square house in the row of square houses that I'd visited; the airline administrator and his cheery wife and athletic son who would become my grandfather, grandmother, and uncle; a story about the local minister, one or two more about her dad's bowling league; something about my mother's first drink when she went off to college. I knew that hers was one of those Midwestern, middle-income, God-fearing, straitlaced households that New York City kids see only on TV reruns. But as she told me more that evening, it all fit into place for the very first time.

I have always thought of my mother as quite rigid. But as she talked, I saw that as natural. After all, she had stretched herself and been stretched from Cleveland to Manhattan, from an all-women's college to an all-male household, Christianity to nothing, her background to mine. I grew up thinking of my mother as bookish, even conservative. But when she described her delight in college life, the thrill of her post-graduate year on scholarship in France, and the wonder of working at a leading New York City literary magazine, I began to fathom her sincere love of learning. But she was stingy, I used to gripe. That's because I had no memory of her working the Christmas rush at Macy's department store, throwing together a catering service with a friend, trying to breed our dog and sell the puppies, and scrambling in a dozen other directions to gather enough money to have three children—until she told me all about it in that pub. Her mode of parenting was not a policy, plot, or random series of notions. She was responding to what she'd lived with, much as I had always responded to her. And her approach to mothering was something I could understand only by approaching her at last.

However, it is not only a knowledge of our pasts that entices us, as we grow older, to make rewarding contact with our moms. Uncertainty about the future can send us motherward as well. Simply aging can strike fear and curiosity into our hearts, breaking down the artificial barriers we've built between our business and our mothers' experiences. Long ago, it came naturally to ask our mothers what our first camp or first grade would be like. Now it happens startlingly, as we approach them with our adult anxieties about what comes next.

The trials and disappointments of aging inspired Phillip, for instance, to turn openly to his mom. In his thirty-seven years, he hadn't spoken to her that way; but after a phone call that featured news of an old friend's death and of changes in his hometown, he was compelled to share his dismay. "I hung up the phone and called my mom," Phillip says. "I didn't even think about it. And I asked her, *Mom, when did you realize that you were middle-aged?* and she said, *Honey, I can tell you the exact minute.* And she did." Phillip and his mother had an ancient history of speaking emotionally, although the practice had petered out somewhere in his adolescence. Now he found himself reviving it, prompted by a discomfort that was both innocent and mature, as well as crucial to an examination of his life.

"When I close my eyes, I see myself as I was when I was twenty-one," Phillip admits. "And I never knew before that my mother does that too. To talk about those passages and those feelings and stages, to be able to say, *Mama, I woke up today and I'm an older man,* and have her say, *Join the club*—that's a very nice thing for me. And it's a whole new side of our relationship that is just going to grow from here."

At forty-one years old, Hugh finds himself having similar feelings and a similar reflex to make genuine contact with his mother. "Over the last five years or so," Hugh says, "the world has really opened up to me. It's hard to describe to a guy who's not there yet. All I can tell you is that everything changed for me during that time, as it changed for other men I know who have gone through that transition." Hugh had found early success, landing a powerful publishing job in his twenties and working hard and profitably ever since. Then he set his sights on making a more internal sort of progress.

"Everything I took for granted was suddenly up for grabs, mentally and emotionally," Hugh describes. "I suddenly wanted to know *everything*: much more than one learns as a matter of course. It was a very interesting state to enter." Hugh was always inquisitive, even as a child. Yet it's only after becoming a veteran at his job, raising two children, and suffering through his father's death that his curiosities have expanded to take on larger questions; questions that are more existential and most often aimed at his mother.

"Lately I've become very interested in thoroughly examining the beginning of my life, as well as changes still to come," he says. "And that's a process that begs for my mother's inclusion. I want to hear about what it's like to be seventy-three. I want to ask my mom, *What's it like?* I never thought about what it would be like to be in my forties, and it turns out to be wonderful. I mean, it's *wonderful*. So I find myself thinking that maybe there's something else wonderful out there, maybe at seventy-three years old. And now I look to her to tell me about it."

A baby boy is an adventurer, crawling and clomping from one investigation to another. A growing boy applies himself more systematically to intellectual pursuits and thus gets through school, moves up in his job, plows forward through relationships. But only as he becomes a reflective man can he coordinate both these approaches and incorporate his mother, in order to turn his queries inward. For a long time, we have affectionately sidelined our moms. Trying to follow a straight path to manhood, an ambitious young man considers a grown woman off-track— until he questions the reasons he's focused on his feet all these years.

Unmaking Tracks

"Listen, Mom, I gotta go."
"Of course. And work is all right? Your father tells me —"

"Fine, uh-huh. So I'd better get moving."
"I know, I know. I just wanted to touch ba—"
"Yep, so, I'm off."
"Okay, honey. But will you do me a favor, and call if you need —"
"You got it. Talk to you soon."
"Now you know that we're going to the —"
"MOM!"

If men sound strangled on the phone with their mothers, that's because they are in something of a vise. As an adult speaking on adult issues to my mom, I behaved this babyishly because I felt squeezed. On one side, I had the pressure dictated by my manly daily life. My efforts and chit-chat were to be made exclusively with colleagues and cohorts; my overall pace was to be maintained at a brisk and consistent level. To ponder emotions, rethink thoughts, and rehash personal trials was too deep and too slow for a guy on the move. Yet that's exactly what my mother was after. When we were on the phone, she was pressing from the other side.

Although she had always supported my hard-edged, hard-working tendencies, my mother now sharply opposed them with her efforts at open and roving conversation. The in-depth talks she was attempting to have were enticing detours and distractions from the straight and narrow. My father knew the anxious time-rationing of men, as he had lived by it himself. He would be on and off the line in six minutes, having completed a list of bulleted points and wishing me well. My mother was less exacting, more alluring, and thus more dangerous. I would have liked to indulge in loose and liberating mother-son exchange. In fact, it was by restraining my desire to do so that I created the pressure of my vise. But I couldn't ease up. I was too swept up in the race, too worried about getting ahead to linger with the woman who was offering to stand behind me.

This is the thin track of the sons of sons of sons, regardless of their characters or career choices. In our attempts to become providers, we proudly deny ourselves. As we work to afford full and rewarding lives, we routinely empty and tax ourselves. And a mother is a large part of what we push away as we push ourselves harder. The thought of unwinding into that age-old friendship, released from severe time constraints and internal shackles, is more than appealing; but the freedom to do so is always a task, accomplishment, or conversation away. Men are under the gun that they hold on themselves.

Despite the growing sense that they can't keep it up forever, sons stay on track. Jack, for instance, has logged more than twenty years in various sales departments. When it comes to taking the daily rigors in stride, he gets winded often; but like all men, he feels the need to keep going. "There are times I'll come home from work, and it's been a rough day, and I've been just crazed the whole time, and I don't want to talk to anyone," Jack says. "I'll be brain dead, even with my own family, and just barely able to watch some dumb TV show or read the paper." During these typical evenings, Jack explains, a phone call from his mother is not odious. But it is unacceptable. "The phone will ring, and my wife will say, *Oh, that'll be your mother, she called earlier.* And I feel bad about this, but every once in a while I'll say, *Tell her I'm not home.*" The reason for Jack's reclusion is not spite or irreverence; as a matter of fact, it's the opposite. "I don't mean to push her away," he says. "I just don't want to get on the phone and give her one-word answers. That's not right, not to your mother. I know she deserves more than that. But a lot of times I just don't have it in me to give her anything more." Men cannot help but become trapped in the pressurized routines that become their lives. However, that does not mean that they aren't eyeing the limits or considering the mothers who represent life beyond their own strict boundaries.

As a young doctor, Brian has lived up to his mother's

hopes for him as her bright and promising only son. Yet he is already aware of the drawbacks of his track. "You have this masculine role that you have to fill," he says. "You're a doctor and you work as hard as you can, make money, don't worry about what it means, hold it all in. But there are other feelings going on. And those are really my mom's department. I'm going all out, career-wise, at this point. But in terms of breaking down in front of someone, I would only feel comfortable doing that in front of my mom." In other words, when it comes to asking the questions that weren't covered in medical school and making the sorts of examinations that don't take place in hospitals, Brian seeks her out. "It's only with my mom that I'll discuss my deeper feelings about being a physician," he says. "Sometimes I can't believe that I'm on my way and that I can handle the pace and all the pressures. She'll hear me out on that and make me feel better. Meanwhile, I'll talk to my dad about the bare-bones facts, like the prospects of being a private practitioner in 1999. And I'll talk to my friends about . . . baseball."

Often, men strive to be busy and independent, until they are inescapably so. It's then that sons, overworked and isolated, stop turning down the invitation of the broader worlds outside their tracks. Some find religions, go bungee jumping, giggle with children, unlearn old habits, and relearn familiar hobbies. Others simply take deep breaths and take themselves quietly out of the race. Their sense of direction becomes less sharply defined, allowing them to sidestep and backtrack freely. Their obsession with pragmatism and efficiency eases to allow for more spontaneous thoughts and more personal pursuits. And the boundary they've drawn between manhood and mothers breaks down as they give in at last to their desires to break it.

When Saul halted his daily grind, he stepped closer to his mom. For years he'd gone full tilt in the entertainment industry. "I did the hard-core, male professional thing," he says. "I did the ulcer thing, where you're always too busy to talk to your mother and you feel like you're working all the time and everyone talks on and on about making it big, whether you are or aren't." But when his father died, his ulcer got worse, his interest in the fast lane sputtered, and Saul opted out. "You're sitting there killing yourself, trying to build as solid a base as you can," he says, "and suddenly I realized that, for me personally, I was sitting on the most jellylike base I knew. It meant nothing to me." Therefore, Saul chose a venture that was more constructive and spiritual. With his inheritance from his father, he decided to build a house in the New Mexican desert.

"My mother understood it immediately," Saul says. "It

was interesting: My stepfather helped me build the house, but he didn't really get it. It was my mom who identified what I was doing. Right off the bat, she saw the symbolism."

Although the project took him from his job and tossed his career options into the air, for Saul it was a most sound and sensible decision. "I was trying to deal with my own psychology," he says. "My father was abusive and an alcoholic, and as a grown man I had to gain independence from all that and build myself some other place. It was just a step sideways for me, but it was an important one. It was an evaluation, not a progressive move forward, a piece of work to change my perspective. And my mother was with me from the very start of it." Saul and his mother met each other halfway: he'd removed himself from business as usual, and she'd moved to support him. "My mom loved the place and loved the act," Saul reflects. Now working more creatively and sporadically across the country, he is pleased to be back in real touch with his mother.

"Your mom knows you better than anyone," he says, "so it didn't surprise me that she really got what I was doing. Nor was I surprised that she was right there, waiting for me, when I'd finally had enough of the macho trenches. But I'll love her forever for how she stuck by me in that transition."

Most of us find ways to meet our mothers offtrack that may be less dramatic, if no less ambitious. "Recently, something's happened between us," says Craig. "I wouldn't have expected it until I turned the corner toward forty, but now it's come to feel natural." What has startled both Craig and his mother is his sudden tendency to telephone her. "I just got the urge to call her one day and take her to lunch," he says. "That was really unusual for me, and not only because I live seventy miles away. She flipped. She kept saying, *Do you have any other reason to come to town?* And I kept saying, *No. I'm coming to take you to lunch.* I would never have done that before." Craig's relationship with his mother has not been particularly smooth or consistent. But in becoming a husband, a father, and a middle-aged man, he has seen his feelings toward her soften and change.

"A funny thing happens as a man gets older—or less young," he considers. "You mellow. You start to think about more things in greater depth. You start to realize that working, eating, and sleeping isn't where it all ends and begins. And you start to embrace your mother. I mean, *really* embrace your mother."

In Craig's opinion, it's all in the hug. When we are young, we hug our mothers quickly, patting them on the back as if to flatten the intimacy. Then the contact becomes more important. "I really want to really mean it, now, when I hug my mom," Craig says. "I don't want to be uncomfortable any more, or embarrassed. I want to show her that I've grown up since the days of that awkwardness, and that I appreciate her." Without all the arm action and percussion, these embraces may look more boring, but the thoughts behind them are more active than ever.

Mature men join their mothers again, not necessarily because their tracks have ended or have led them there, but because they realize that they never will. We have kept our mothers at arm's length in order to apply ourselves fully and individually to our business, to keep up our pace, and to secure a sense of accomplishment. But eventually, most men snap out of it, either by remembering the satisfaction of fully engaging with their moms, or by forgetting why they have deferred it for so long.

My mother arrived on time and flopped on my couch. I sank into the chair across from her. After spending a long weekend with my brother Luke, then the floor manager of a rock club, she had a slew of stories. I had just spoken to Jake in Moscow and filled her in on the progress of the health club he's founded. I got us food from the fridge, and we yammered on. She'd come up with a great idea for a biography, and we debated whether or not the subject had been covered. I was having a hell of a time interviewing teenage boys, and we brainstormed on how to pry them open. Before I knew it she'd stood up: Her train would be leaving in only a few minutes. I walked her toward the door—and she froze. "Shoot—we didn't even go over mother-and-son stuff," she said. "I'm sorry, was I talking . . ." She eyed me with her hand to her head. I cringed too; and then I laughed. The scheduled interview hadn't taken place. I wasn't even sure where my tape recorder was, and didn't much care. We had not talked mothers and sons, it was true. Instead, a mother and son had just talked.

Such afternoons may be uneventful, but they are remarkable for that reason. For all our ambition, we young men usually are incapable of such astounding feats as sitting with our mothers—no agenda, no schedule, just us. Our maturity allows for mother-to-man connections that, until they're made, we must have assumed were too hard, or perhaps too easy. And these connections, in time, bring a gentle reversal of roles.

Mothering Our Moms

I find myself telling people about her, gabbing to friends and strangers, glowing as I recount her accomplishments: *You've seen her books, I'm sure. Haven't you? The article, of course, was much longer, even better, before they cut it. She's thinking of starting a biography—but I shouldn't say anything. Big, suffice it to say. Very big.* And what she hasn't achieved, I encourage her to attempt. I've pumped her with thoughts of poetry, maybe a memoir. When she mentioned a new writing project, I bought her a fancy notebook. When she talked of research in France, I bought her an old novel about Paris. I give her advice on the politics of publishing that she most likely knows already. I pass along the names of magazine contacts who are younger and less powerful than the people she's in touch with. I am acting proud and doting and as supportive as I can—and more like a stereotypical mother than she's ever acted with me.

When the organic bond between men and their mothers is no longer kept secret, when rocket men at last touch down and silent sons find their voices, what is revealed is unexpected. Not only have we been paying attention to our mothers all our lives; we have learned to behave as mothers toward them. Mature men outwardly support their moms' individual goals, applaud their developments, and seek to take care of them, just as their mothers did long ago for them. These are not the muted ponderings of the tight-lipped nor the underground feelings of the sons who act oppositely. These are the wholehearted speeches and devoted actions of sons who have dropped their getups, tired of their folklore, and entered true manhood by paying more attention to their mothers than to how men are supposed to act.

In the same way that a mom fostered her son's ambitions, a grown son gives his mother a boost in any way he can. "I worry terribly that my mother has squandered her gift," says Ryan. "She should be out there making use of it, making more of herself with her ability." What leaves Ryan fuming and egging his mother on is that ten years ago, at the age of fifty-five, she gave up playing the piano. Once a concert musician, she has barely touched the instrument since, and while she invents long strings of excuses—being out of practice, not wanting to disturb neighbors—Ryan is unrelenting.

"I've asked her many times to pick it up again," he says. "I would love for her grandchildren to know her as the artist she is. It would be liberating for her to get back into the instrument. But I think she's scared. She's climbed into a sort of shell and is afraid of what she'll find if she tries again." Like a zealous mother, Ryan understands her hesitancy but refuses to accept it.

"If you listen to her old performances, she was an extraordinarily graceful, vivid, sensual musician," he says. "Her passion came through the keyboard. She should let herself come out that way again. I'm angry that she gave up the piano at a point, regardless of her age, when she was just hitting her stride."

Without his mother's knowing it, Paul has watched over her personal progress for years. When Paul was growing up, his father traveled often, leaving his mom with household-management duties that kept her from other pursuits. Now that her three children have their own lives, though, she has the potential to do anything. And now that Paul is an adult, he feels free to tell her so. "She's always been, in a sense, a captive of her lifestyle and a prisoner—though not literally—of our family," Paul considers. "For as long as I can remember, my mother never took a trip. My dad and the rest of us did all we could for ourselves, running around and traveling for business and pleasure; but not her. So now I feel the need to bug her about that."

Even more important than globe-trotting, Paul thinks, would be a long-delayed profession. "Occasionally my mom will joke, *Maybe I'll start a restaurant.* And I'm always like, *Yeah! That's a great idea!*" he says. "But then she sort of forgets about it and lets it drop. Meanwhile, I don't want to let those things pass any longer. I want her to go out and find happiness, exercise herself the way the rest of us got to. If I had any money, I would fund it myself. I would help her if she wanted my help. But of course, she doesn't."

It's not easy to thrust a loved one into the world. A son knows that lesson well, and now from both sides. He can, however, derive gratification from watching his mother's step-by-step development. He celebrates her ability to change and progress with a delight that rivals that of new parents. He monitors her growth and applauds her blossoming as if she were speaking her first words, taking her first steps—and in the event that those are aimed toward him, his pride and joy are uncontainable.

I'm not sure when, where, or how my Africa thing began. There's a scrapbook I made at eight years old that features safari images torn from *National Geographic,* and that artifact may hold clues as to why, a decade later, I shipped myself spontaneously to Ghana. A couple years after that, it was a few months in Kenya and Tanzania. Then a year in Botswana and South Africa, a quick trip to Zimbabwe, a drive through Namibia, a return visit to rural Kenya and the eastern coast of the continent. I majored in sub-Saharan anthropology, learned handfuls of several languages, did undergraduate work at an African university and graduate work in two more. Ethiopia, however, was a country I never saw. To my surprise, that was left to my mother.

She is not the homebody type, nor a stranger to airplanes or foreign landscapes. But *Africa*? While she is an old hand at Parisian cafés and can order anything in small-town Italy, this seemed something of a stretch. But my mother told me the news without drama: She was to serve as a journalist during an all-women human rights tour of Eritrea. I had twinges of worry and an urge to issue warnings, but more than any other impulse I had, I was tremendously pleased. Ten years before, when I'd announced my first African expedition, her face had dropped. Now she was grinning at the thought of her few weeks there. She had expanded and was reaching out farther and farther. She had taken her cue from an ever-shrinking world and her ever-growing son, and I felt a rush of admiration that doubled upon her triumphant return. My mother was evolving, and in that daring process she was doing me proud.

.   .   .

"My mother has really gone through some big changes," says Jeffrey, "and to watch her take them on the way she has, that just floods me with happiness." When his father died, long after he and his siblings had moved away, Jeffrey worried for his mom—but not for long. She got a job on the *Mayflower*, to her son's surprise, working as a tour guide for visitors to the famous docked ship. And by the time Jeffrey had become assustomed to this news, his mom surprised him in other ways.

"She let go of a lot of the old prejudices that she'd always carried around," he says. "She used to be very scornful of people, very aware of class and comportment, and snobby in her opinions of other walks of life. But suddenly this wide range of people was walking by her every day, tourists of all races and from all over the world. And by simply confronting the human parade in every shape and size, every color, every language, obese, obnoxious, and whatever else, she was broken down in a truly great way."

Over the years, Jeffrey and his mother had waged head-to-head battles over what he felt was her indefensible bigotry and what she felt was his hippy softness. But as she cultivated a new and more progressive life for herself, his mom also evoked her son's deep respect. "She really saw for the first time what I was arguing for way back then," he says, "which is that people are people are people and you can't sniff and turn up your nose at them. It took a lot for her to learn a lesson that big. It took strength."

Although his mother did not officially cede any earlier debates, her new actions and attitudes spoke far more movingly than words. "To see her change like that showed me that she was a powerful person, a strong and good soul," Jeffrey says. "I could actually watch it happen, watch her develop before my eyes, like I must have developed before her eyes. And it amazed me."

Not all mothers' sons progress briskly or on schedule, and not all sons' mothers do either. Pete's frustration with his mom is a common one: a parental-sounding complaint that she's bent on disobedience, doomed not to catch on and to fall far behind. "I can talk to her until I die about the dos and don'ts of how to deal with me and deal with her life," he says, "but what I've come to realize, as I've become an adult, is that with her it goes in one ear and out the other. She might listen, but she doesn't take any action. Based on what I've seen with her, you can't get your mother to follow your lead and keep developing. You just can't." Pete would like his mom to seek wider-ranging friendships, greater job security, and even a new husband, and is dismayed at her reluctance to do so. His emotions are a mixture of concern and offense, as he worries about her inability to be proactive and laments that he cannot inspire her.

"As my relationship with her has gone along, the roles have reversed," Pete acknowledges. "That's what happens. But in my experience, the new dynamic doesn't quite work. The son can't teach the mother. The mother instills certain values in her son; but as he turns into an adult and sees problems with his mother and tries to get her to correct them, it doesn't happen. And that, for me, has been a fairly major letdown."

Thus aging boys are welcomed to the other side of mother-son diplomacy, the quiet push and pull they once took part in without much thought. Now that we have finally grounded ourselves and opened our minds and mouths, many of our mothers appear to put themselves out of reach. Caught in the thrill of ambitious conversation, we are hurt when our moms seem less than thrilled to chime in. Sons have returned from within themselves to meet their mothers in all candor, and it's painful to be greeted by her absence. Of course, it should not be surprising when such reconnections take time. But to men looking for linkage, it comes as a disappointment.

"I'm not going to sit there forever and talk about which restaurants she went to last week," declares Cliff. "I'm not going to chatter endlessly about how my cute children are coming along. A whole range of personal issues have come to be important to me, and all of them are things that she won't talk about." It's only in the last few years that Cliff has become so assertive; but with more than forty complacent years behind him and an elderly mother before him, he is unwilling to wait a few more. "I'm looking to have a relationship with her where I can discuss real things, adult-to-adult. And apparently that's just not something that she's willing to do with me. So I'm beginning to stop trying. What I've learned is that life's too short and too rich, and there's too much, just too much."

In spite of his exasperation, Cliff feels sad more than anything else. "I see her turning into someone who truly does not want to know things," he says. "She doesn't want new information. She's becoming a person who wants to know if the kids called without really caring what we say when we call. I, on the other hand, am more interested than I've ever been in exploring what's been unexplored in our lives. But she doesn't want to join me in that. So I communicate with her less these days."

The exchanging of roles that comes with age is neither a silent switch nor a perfect click. As sons act like mothers and mothers like sons, they both are off-balance, and many men are sent reeling. Sons once winced at personal questions and wriggled away from responding; now they learn the pain of being struck by that same silence. As boys, they disliked their mothers' fretting and shrugged off the pampering, but now that men want to take care of their mothers, they find that even more difficult—and increasingly awkward as their moms age.

My mom used to jog every day, very first thing. At 7:00 A.M. she'd be sweating lightly over our English muffins, four miles under her belt, when we were just starting to dress ourselves for school. She was beyond me, I used to feel. She went before me, checking out the whole neighborhood at a brisk clip hours before I set a groggy foot in the driveway. And I enjoyed her groundbreaking strength. More than anything else, my mother's daily runs showed me that she could escape but chose to return. She had her own pace and power, hidden urges that woke her up and hurtled her outdoors. She had her very own route that brought her, flushed and stronger, back to us by breakfast time.

But a few years ago the pavement-pounding began to take its toll. She didn't admit it at first, scoffing at some stupid twinge in her back that surely would go away, a drag for a day or two. In fact, it was a painful case of degenerative discs. Then her hip began to hurt, lacking enough cartilage to keep the joint moving without friction even as she continued to jog. Inevitable, her doctors sighed: a simple symptom of age. She was talked into stretching drills and rest—which, these days, she interprets to mean shorter distances, maybe an occasional day off. And while she laughs at herself, contorted before the couch in pre-scribed exercises, I grimace to myself. She now faces a hip-replacement operation that she's stubbornly put off. I, meanwhile, face the awful knowledge that there's noth-ing I can do for her. My mother is not getting old yet, de-spite her years, regardless of her ailments. Someone that good at pacing and pushing herself cannot be over the hill. But she is not good at aging. And I am not good at pre-venting it.

If men could secure their mothers from the quiet on-slaught of years, they would. Neil, for instance, comes as close as he possibly can, after decades of honing his tech-nique. While he can't change the fact of his mother's in-creasing memory loss, he can at least cushion her feelings about it.

"My mom has this sense that she's losing her mind," Neil says, "and she does get forgetful. It's just age, as they say: If I'm a half-century old, then she's up there." After a lifetime of closeness between an only child and his only mother, Neil embraces his assignment as his mother's keeper. Yet he is pained by it as well. "So what I've decided to do," he says, "is to pretend that I've forgotten something every time I'm around her. When she blanks on something, I'll try to lowball her on it by forgetting something too. Like: *What the devil did I do with my keys?* You see. Sometimes I'll even say, *Man, I think that I'm losing my mind.* I've gotten to be a pretty good actor." Lacking surgical precision and medical expertise, sons cannot defend their mothers' bodies, but they can take a shot at their spirits. "I'm not trying to fool her into some sort of healing," Neil explains. "I do it because I really don't want her to feel bad. I *need* her not to feel bad, for the sake of my own heart, more and more."

Having arrived at middle age and watched his mother sneak toward old age, Ron expresses his caretaking impulses in a different way: in anger. "Every new disease that's on the news, she's got it," he snaps. "And every new medicine, she wants it. It's a common joke about Jewish mothers, that they play the martyr, but it's true. She complains all the time." However, it's Ron's disposition, more than his mom's personality, that makes her moanings so personally upsetting for him.

Ron sees himself as wholly responsible for his mother, a stance that leaves him easily and painfully knocked over. "I mean, what am I supposed to do?" he exclaims. "I live six hours away. I'm married. I have children. I have problems of my own. I can't just run over there and save the day because her feet hurt again or her eyes are doing 'that thing.' " Complaints give way to accusations as Ron vents his pain in response to hers. "She doesn't even want her problems solved," he says. "She'd rather have them again and again. It gives her something to talk about." More notable than the frequency of her medical claims is the passion with which Ron rails against them. A mother's suffering, whether real or imagined, means a lapse in the duty that sons have assigned themselves.

Grown-up sons may be accustomed to their wives and children, seasoned at their jobs, and accomplished in their realms; but they are no experts when it comes to caring for their caretaker of decades before. They are armed only with unanswered queries and private frowns, clever put-ons and halfhearted gripes, and a fundamental affection that is hard to demonstrate. Therefore it comes as a profound relief when they can take concrete action in the service of their mothers. A young boy leaps at the chance to battle someone on his mother's behalf; an older boy lashes out at the thought that his mother could be replaced; and a full-grown man steps gratefully to his mother's side when she finally needs his help.

Steven has not always seemed eager to do so. He was a sullen child, a "sour puss," he admits, "who wouldn't give my mother the time of day." His teenage years were erratic: "It was like my mom didn't exist," he recalls, "unless I needed her for some self-serving reason." And his early adulthood was something of a disappearing act: "I was traveling a lot, for my job, and hardly ever got the chance to call my mom," Steven explains. "But to be honest, it wasn't just that. There hadn't been much for me at home. It wasn't anyone's fault, really, but there were a couple divorces, and my mom was sad a lot of the time, and there wasn't much of a sense of home to engage me. So I suppose I kind of turned my back on her." However, now that he's in his early forties and his mother's been weakened by illness, Steven has changed course by adopting the full-time care of her.

"It's probably hard for you to understand, at your age," he tells me. "I wouldn't have understood it. But when my mom got sick, it was, in an odd way, a gift for me. It was a chance to show her, plain and simple, that I had cared about her all my life and would care for her quite literally now." Without any complex negotiations, with no awkwardness or long debates about the past, Steven was pleased to take her into his home—and thus show her, in simple fashion, that she had essentially been there all along.

Although Steven is wholly content, he is not entirely

correct. I do know the feeling, if not the action. Like all young men, I am suspended in the years between being attended to by my mother and being able to return the favor. Like the sons of this story, I look back with gratitude, look forward with eagerness, and look to my mother with more feeling than she could know. I have written this book in many voices and with many emotions, every one of them mine, all the hundreds of them hers. And until I can come up with more, I give this to the woman who gave me myself.

CONCLUSION

THERE ARE VARIOUS THEORIES CONCERNING THE point at which one actually becomes a writer. Some enthusiasts maintain that you need only to have put earnest pen to paper, scrapped efforts included. Many contend that it's once you're published; more say that it's once you're paid; and still others confer the title only on those who have arrived at doing absolutely nothing else. As for me, I anointed myself a writer when I was approximately six. This dementia undoubtedly took hold as I became aware of my mother's career as a journalist, editor, and author. I must have inherited her vocation as I inherited her looks. In more ways than one, I have taken after my mom. Or rather, I have not.

This is my first book. More remarkable than that, this

is the first time ever that I have sought out my mother's input on any writing project of any shape or size, from compositions as a nine-year-old to essays in national magazines. In the past year I have turned to her with research questions and narrative tangles, and she has responded with an expertise that I have never known, and that has always been seconds away. Quite honestly, I hadn't thought to seek it. Sure, we both happened to write, I figured, in the same way that we both *spoke*; but our accents and audiences were different. No, more than that—*I* was different. I was a young man and she was an older woman. I planned to be louder, funnier, and to broadcast farther than she could, in the way men do. But make no mistake: There wasn't any sense of competition. To compete, we would have to be side-by-side. And my mother and I—with the same chin, the same memories, and the same lifelong ambition—were on entirely different paths.

We converged at my parents' house for the first official handoff of pages. I felt stiff, defensive. She didn't say much, just riffled the bottom edge of the stack and put it on her bedside table with an assurance that she'd get to it soon. I was impressed already. *You're going to let your mom read it as you go?* my friends laughed. *Did she stipulate that in your book contract? Was that your Mother's Day gift? She must be chomping at the bit.* It was a few long days before I heard anything. In fact, I heard little—but read plenty: her comments scrolled in cursive across several yellow sheets of legal paper, corresponding page and line numbers jotted in the right margin. *Does your mommy give you big smiley stickers on every page?* people teased me. Not exactly: Rewrite notices marred the manuscript, penciled lines slashed through whole paragraphs, underlined instructions told me to speed it up, slow it down, cut all this dull preamble, be *honest* here. *You're going to kill your poor mom. She's going to cry when you tell the world about her back pain. She'll have a heart attack when you talk about kissing her good night.* My mother starred these sections and urged more detail. I called my editor to explain that I might need a bit more time.

The longer and harder I worked on the book, the greater my resolve to get to the heart of mother-son issues; and, oddly, to get to my mother. Countless sons had complained to me on tape about their mothers' excessive emotions and lack of objectivity. To my surprise, I was witnessing the opposite—and this constituted a challenge. Somewhere in the process of scrawling, typing, handing it over, and getting it back, I decided that if I could get my mother to shed her editorial armor and respond like a mom, I'd done it.

A minor coup occurred after a few weeks, when she confessed to being "moved" at one point in one paragraph in chapter 1. I managed another small triumph in chapter 3, after two or three drafts, when she sounded a note of maternal discomfort: "I did *not* plan a volleyball game for your graduation party," she insisted over the phone, then laughed. "The net was there for, um, shade." She began to call me more often than usual. I noticed that she was posing more questions about my goings-on than she had for years. Finally with chapter 5 came victory. It was my father who sounded the trumpet, in a whisper over the telephone. "Your mother cried," he told me, his hand cupping the phone. "She was reading it out loud to me, and she teared up. I saw her."

But my mother hardly fell apart. On the contrary, she held her son and his manuscript together and made us both ambitious. Without her inspiration, this book would not have been written. Without her skills and intelligence, it would not have been particularly interesting. And without the arrival of such an urgent and daunting project, she and I might never have learned what we've known, quite naturally, all along: that a boy may take after his mother in order to thrive as a man. Mothers and sons can grow up without growing apart, and can prove themselves separate people without clumsily insisting on separating themselves. We men can have far more in common with the women who raised us than the odd physical feature and a few hidden personality quirks. We may share even our lives.

ACKNOWLEDGMENTS

This book would not have been started if it weren't for the wisdom of Susan Petersen, and it would not have been completed if it weren't for the following people, whose help I very gratefully acknowledge:

Jane Isay, for her editorial expertise; Mary South, for her sharp insight and deep friendship; Kathryn Crosby, for her hard work; my entire extended family at Riverhead Books and Putnam, for giving me a lasting home; Gloria Loomis, for her faith and knowledge; my father, Davis, for his vigilant support; my brothers, Jake and Luke, for their permanent fellowship; and Amanda Beesley, for her brains, her patience, and my sanity.

In addition to those who helped deliver this book, I would like to thank the hundreds of boys and men who helped create it. By spending time and energy putting their lives into words, they are the ones who truly wrote *The Secret Love of Sons* for their mothers.

Finally, I am vastly indebted to my own mother, Elizabeth Hawes Weinstock, for her hard and generous work in shaping every page of this book and every one of her sons. I am lucky to have her behind me, but I am improved by having her before me.